Learning OpenTelemetry
Setting Up and Operating a Modern Observability System

Ted Young and Austin Parker

Beijing · Boston · Farnham · Sebastopol · Tokyo

Learning OpenTelemetry

by Ted Young and Austin Parker

Copyright © 2024 Ted Young and Austin Parker. All rights reserved.

Published by O'Reilly Media, Inc., 1005 Gravenstein Highway North, Sebastopol, CA 95472.

O'Reilly books may be purchased for educational, business, or sales promotional use. Online editions are also available for most titles (*http://oreilly.com*). For more information, contact our corporate/institutional sales department: 800-998-9938 or *corporate@oreilly.com*.

Acquisitions Editor: John Devins
Development Editor: Sarah Grey
Production Editor: Aleeya Rahman
Copyeditor: Arthur Johnson
Proofreader: Sharon Wilkey

Indexer: nSight, Inc.
Interior Designer: David Futato
Cover Designer: Karen Montgomery
Illustrator: Kate Dullea

March 2024:   First Edition

Revision History for the First Edition
2024-03-05:   First Release

See *http://oreilly.com/catalog/errata.csp?isbn=9781098147181* for release details.

978-1-098-14718-1

[LSI]

For Dylan Mae

—Austin

For the OpenTelemetry cofounders

—Ted

Table of Contents

Foreword

In the ever-evolving landscape of cloud-native technologies, observing an application's performance and health is no longer a luxury, but a critical imperative. As microservice architectures become the norm, distributed systems sprawl, and data volumes explode, traditional monitoring tools struggle to keep pace. This is where OpenTelemetry emerges as a game changer, offering a standardized and vendor-neutral approach to observability. OpenTelemetry is not just a technology; it also represents a paradigm shift, "crossing the chasm" from just monitoring to complete observability. OpenTelemetry is changing the industry from silos to unified telemetry.

As the authors Ted Young and Austin Parker explain, OpenTelemetry is about embracing a unified telemetry data-driven approach to observability, leveraging open standards like the OpenTelemetry Protocol (OTLP), and being empowered to build and operate fully observable, resilient, high-performing cloud-native applications.

Learning OpenTelemetry serves as your comprehensive guide to unlocking the power of OpenTelemetry. Whether you're a seasoned engineer grappling with the complexities of distributed tracing, a newcomer seeking to understand the fundamentals, or an organization embarking on its observability journey, this book equips you with the knowledge and practical insights to navigate this transformative technology.

The authors emphasize that observability requires understanding the cloud-native paradigm's broader context and inherent challenges. For example, microservice architectures, while offering agility and scalability, introduce new complexities. Traditional monitoring tools, designed for monolithic applications, often struggle to capture the intricate interactions and dependencies between services. This lack of coherent visibility leads to visibility gaps, making it difficult to pinpoint performance bottlenecks, diagnose issues, and ensure application health.

Learning OpenTelemetry highlights how OpenTelemetry addresses these challenges head-on by providing a unified and vendor-agnostic approach to collecting and exporting telemetry data. This unified approach uses metrics, traces, logs, and profiling to offer a correlated view of your application's health and performance.

The authors delve into the intricacies of OpenTelemetry, guiding us through core concepts of OpenTelemetry and pursuing instrumentation strategies for different programming languages and frameworks such as shared libraries and shared services. They illuminate best practices for collecting and processing telemetry data using the OpenTelemetry Collector; they survey deployment patterns for scaling telemetry collection for platforms such as Kubernetes, serverless and data streaming. They'll show you how to build scalable telemetry pipelines by balancing wide approaches with deep ones, centralized architectures with decentralized ones, and more. The final chapter explores advanced topics, such as generative AI, FinOps, and cloud sustainability.

We live in exciting times. As the worlds of cloud-native services and AI applications converge, it's critical to use telemetry data to understand large-scale model behavior. That's why the next giant leap in OpenTelemetry's journey will be to provide an open framework to fully support observability for smart, distributed GenAI applications. Observability, as a practice, must incorporate viable AI models to collect and analyze telemetry at massive scale.

So, open this book, dive into the world of OpenTelemetry, and unlock the power of observability for your cloud-native journey. Remember, the path to mastery starts with a single step, and this book is a guide to your first and following steps in that journey.

Enjoy!

— Alolita Sharma
Palo Alto, California
February 2024

Alolita Sharma is an OpenTelemetry Governance Committee member and has been contributing to the OpenTelemetry project for over five years. She is co-chair for the CNCF Observability Technical Advisory Group (TAG) and leads Apple's AIML observability practice. She contributes to open source and open standards in OpenTelemetry, Observability TAG, Unicode and W3C. Alolita has also provided strong leadership for observability, infrastructure, and search engineering at AWS and has managed engineering teams at IBM, PayPal, Twitter, and Wikipedia.

Preface

Over the past decade, observability has gone from a niche discipline talked about at events like Monitorama or Velocity (RIP) to a multibillion-dollar industry that touches every part of the cloud native world. The key to effective observability, though, is high-quality telemetry data. OpenTelemetry is a project that aims to provide this data and, in doing so, kick off the next generation of observability tools and practices.

If you're reading this book, it's highly likely that you're an observability practitioner—perhaps a developer or an SRE—who is interested in how to profile and understand complex systems in production. You may have picked it up because you're interested in what OpenTelemetry *is*, how it fits together, and what makes it different from historical monitoring frameworks. Or maybe you're just trying to understand what all the hype is about. After all, in just five years, OpenTelemetry has gone from an idea to one of the most popular open source projects in the world. Regardless of why you're here, we're glad you came.

Our goal in writing this book was not to create a "missing manual" for OpenTelemetry—you can find lots of documentation and tutorials and several other fantastic books that dive deep into implementing OpenTelemetry in specific languages (see Appendix B for details on those). Our goal was to present a comprehensive guide to *learning* OpenTelemetry itself. We want you to understand not just what the different parts are but how they fit together and *why*. This book should equip you with the foundational knowledge you'll need not only to implement OpenTelemetry in a production system but also to extend OpenTelemetry itself—either as a contributor to the project or by making it part of an organizational observability strategy.

In general, this book has two main parts. In Chapters 1 through 4, we discuss the current state of monitoring and observability and show you the motivation behind OpenTelemetry. These chapters help you understand the foundational concepts that underpin the entire project. They're invaluable not just for first-time readers but for anyone who's been practicing observability for a while. Chapters 5 through 9 move into specific use cases and implementation strategies. We discuss the "how" behind the concepts introduced in earlier chapters and give you pointers on actually implementing OpenTelemetry in a variety of applications and scenarios.

If you're already well versed in observability topics, you might be considering skipping ahead to the latter part of the book. While we can't stop you, you'll probably get something out of reviewing the initial chapters. Regardless, as long as you go into this book with an open mind, you should get something out of it—and keep coming back, time after time. We hope this book becomes the foundation for the next chapter of *your* observability journey.

Conventions Used in This Book

The following typographical conventions are used in this book:

Italic
> Indicates new terms, URLs, email addresses, filenames, and file extensions.

`Constant width`
> Used for program listings, as well as within paragraphs to refer to program elements such as variable or function names, databases, data types, environment variables, statements, and keywords.

`Constant width bold`
> Shows commands or other text that should be typed literally by the user.

`Constant width italic`
> Shows text that should be replaced with user-supplied values or by values determined by context.

 This element signifies a tip or suggestion.

 This element signifies a general note.

 This element indicates a warning or caution.

Using Code Examples

Supplemental material (code examples, exercises, etc.) is available for download at *https://github.com/orgs/learning-opentelemetry-oreilly/*.

If you have a technical question or a problem using the code examples, please send email to *support@oreilly.com*.

This book is here to help you get your job done. In general, if example code is offered with this book, you may use it in your programs and documentation. You do not need to contact us for permission unless you're reproducing a significant portion of the code. For example, writing a program that uses several chunks of code from this book does not require permission. Selling or distributing examples from O'Reilly books does require permission. Answering a question by citing this book and quoting example code does not require permission. Incorporating a significant amount of example code from this book into your product's documentation does require permission.

We appreciate, but generally do not require, attribution. An attribution usually includes the title, author, publisher, and ISBN. For example: "*Learning OpenTelemetry* by Ted Young and Austin Parker (O'Reilly). Copyright 2024 Austin Parker and Ted Young, 9781098147181."

If you feel your use of code examples falls outside fair use or the permission given above, feel free to contact us at *permissions@oreilly.com*.

O'Reilly Online Learning

 For more than 40 years, *O'Reilly Media* has provided technology and business training, knowledge, and insight to help companies succeed.

Our unique network of experts and innovators share their knowledge and expertise through books, articles, and our online learning platform. O'Reilly's online learning platform gives you on-demand access to live training courses, in-depth learning paths, interactive coding environments, and a vast collection of text and video from O'Reilly and 200+ other publishers. For more information, visit *https://oreilly.com*.

How to Contact Us

Please address comments and questions concerning this book to the publisher:

O'Reilly Media, Inc.
1005 Gravenstein Highway North
Sebastopol, CA 95472
800-889-8969 (in the United States or Canada)
707-827-7019 (international or local)
707-829-0104 (fax)
support@oreilly.com
https://www.oreilly.com/about/contact.html

We have a web page for this book, where we list errata, examples, and any additional information. You can access this page at *https://oreil.ly/learning-opentelemetry*.

For news and information about our books and courses, visit *https://oreilly.com*.

Find us on LinkedIn: *https://linkedin.com/company/oreilly-media*

Watch us on YouTube: *https://youtube.com/oreillymedia*

Acknowledgments

The authors would like to thank their entire team at O'Reilly for constant support, encouragement, and grace. Special thanks go out to our acquisitions editor, John Devins, and our developmental editor, Sarah Grey. We also thank our tech reviewers for their invaluable feedback, as well as Alolita Sharma for her contribution.

This book would not be possible without the work of every OpenTelemetry contributor across the years.

Austin

I'd like to thank my coauthor for convincing me that writing another book would be a good idea, actually.

To my partner, Mandy: thank you for putting up with the long hours and unpredictable nature of writing. *Tada gan iarracht.*[1]

I would also like to thank the many people whom I used as sounding boards over the past year or so, and whose friendship and ideas have made it into these words; they include (but are not limited to) Phillip Carter, Alex Hidalgo, Jessica Kerr, Reese Lee,

---

1 "Nothing without effort."

Rynn Mancuso, Ana Margarita Medina, Ben Sigelman, Pierre Tessier, Amy Tobey, Adriana Villela, Hazel Weakly, and Christine Yen. All y'all great humans.

Ted

I'd like to thank my coauthor for being convinced that writing another book would be a good idea, actually.

I would like to thank all the maintainers of the OpenTracing and OpenCensus projects. Both projects have the same goal: to create a universal standard for describing the computer operations of distributed systems. Choosing to put egos aside, merge the projects, and accept a years-long setback as we started over with OpenTelemetry was a difficult decision. I appreciate the bravery and trust that it took to do this.

I would also like to thank the maintainers of the Elastic Common Schema project. This was another case in which having two standards meant that we had no standards. Their willingness to merge ECS into the OpenTelemetry Semantic Conventions was another important step toward our shared goal of a universally accepted telemetry system.

It's a common (and funny) joke to point at OpenTelemetry and bring up the classic *XKCD* comic #927, "How Standards Proliferate" (*https://xkcd.com/927*). But I must say, *au contraire, Monsieur chuckles!* OpenTelemetry did create a new standard, but in the process it deprecated three other standards. So we are now at minus two standards. I believe this may be a record in the history of standardization. I'm hoping for at least minus four before we're done.

CHAPTER 1

The State of Modern Observability

History is not the past but a map of the past, drawn from a particular point of view, to be useful to the modern traveler.

— Henry Glassie, US historian[1]

This is a book about the difficult problems inherent to large-scale distributed computer systems, and about how to apply OpenTelemetry to help solve those problems.

Modern software engineering is obsessed with end-user experience, and end users demand blazing-fast performance. Surveys show that users will abandon ecommerce sites that take more than two seconds to load (*https://oreil.ly/tZ9tY*). You've probably spent a fair amount of time trying to optimize and debug application performance issues, and if you're like us, you've been frustrated by how inelegant and inefficient this process can be. There's either not enough data or too much of it, and what data there is can be riddled with inconsistencies or unclear measurements.

Engineers are also faced with stringent uptime requirements. That means identifying and mitigating any issues before they cause a meltdown, not just waiting for the system to fail. And it means moving quickly from triage to mitigation. To do that, you need data.

But you don't need just any data; you need *correlated data*—data that is already organized, ready to be analyzed by a computer system. As you will see, data with that level of organization has not been readily available. In fact, as systems have scaled and become more heterogeneous, finding the data you need to analyze an issue has become even harder. If it was once like looking for a needle in a haystack, it's now more like looking for a needle in a stack of needles.

---

1 Henry Glassie, *Passing the Time in Ballymenone: Culture and History of an Ulster Community* (Philadelphia: University of Pennsylvania Press, 1982).

OpenTelemetry solves this problem. By turning individual logs, metrics, and traces into a coherent, unified graph of information, OpenTelemetry sets the stage for the next generation of observability tools. And since the software industry is broadly adopting OpenTelemetry already, that next generation of tools is being built as we write this.

The Times They Are A-Changin'

Technology comes in waves. As we write this in 2024, the field of observability is riding its first real tsunami in at least 30 years. You've chosen a good time to pick up this book and gain a new perspective!

The advent of cloud computing and cloud native application systems has led to seismic shifts in the practice of building and operating complex software systems. What hasn't changed, though, is that software runs on computers, and you need to understand what those computers are doing in order to understand your software. As much as the cloud has sought to abstract away fundamental units of computing, our ones and zeros are still using bits and bytes.

Whether you are running a program on a multiregion Kubernetes cluster or a laptop, you will find yourself asking the same questions:

> "Why is it slow?"
> "What is using so much RAM?"
> "When did this problem start?"
> "Where is the root cause?"
> "How do I fix this?"

The astronomer and science communicator Carl Sagan said, "You have to know the past to understand the present."[2] That certainly applies here: to see why a new approach to observability is so important, you first need to be familiar with traditional observability architecture and its limitations.

This may look like a recap of rudimentary information! But the observability mess has been around for so long that most of us have developed quite the pile of preconceptions. So even if you're an expert—*especially* if you're an expert—it is important to have a fresh perspective. Let's start this journey by defining several key terms we will use throughout this book.

---

2 Carl E. Sagan (author and presenter), in *Cosmos: A Personal Voyage*, season 1, episode 2, "One Voice in the Cosmic Fugue," produced by Adrian Malone (Arlington, VA: Public Broadcasting Service, 1980).

Observability: Key Terms to Know

First of all, what is observability observing? For the purposes of this book, we are observing distributed systems. A *distributed system* is a system whose components are located on different networked computers that communicate and coordinate their actions by passing messages to one another.[3] There are many kinds of computer systems, but these are the ones we're focusing on.

What Counts as Distributed?

Distributed systems aren't just applications running in the cloud, microservices, or Kubernetes applications. Macroservices or "monoliths" that use service-oriented architecture, client applications that communicate with a backend, and mobile and web apps are all somewhat distributed and benefit from observability.

At the highest level, a distributed system consists of resources and transactions:

Resources
> These are all the physical and logical components that make up a system. *Physical components*, such as servers, containers, processes, RAM, CPU, and network cards, are all resources. *Logical components*, such as clients, applications, API endpoints, databases, and load balancers, are also resources. In short, resources are everything from which the system is actually constructed.

Transactions
> These are requests that orchestrate and utilize the resources the system needs to do work on behalf of the user. Usually, a transaction is kicked off by a real human, who is waiting for the task to be completed. Booking a flight, hailing a rideshare, and loading a web page are examples of transactions.

How do we observe these distributed systems? We can't, unless they emit telemetry. *Telemetry* is data that describes what your system is doing. Without telemetry, your system is just a big black box filled with mystery.

Many developers find the word *telemetry* confusing. It's an overloaded term. The distinction we draw in this book, and in systems monitoring in general, is between user telemetry and performance telemetry:

---

3 Andrew S. Tanenbaum and Maarten van Steen, *Distributed Systems: Principles and Paradigms* (Upper Saddle River, NJ: Prentice Hall, 2002).

User telemetry

Refers to data about how a user is interacting with a system through a client: button clicks, session duration, information about the client's host machine, and so forth. You can use this data to understand how users are interacting with an ecommerce site, or the distribution of browser versions accessing a web-based application.

Performance telemetry

This is not primarily used to analyze user behavior; instead, it provides operators with statistical information about the behavior and performance of system components. Performance data can come from different sources in a distributed system and offers developers a "breadcrumb trail" to follow, connecting cause with effect.

In plainer terms, user telemetry will tell you how long someone hovered their mouse cursor over a Checkout button in an ecommerce application. Performance telemetry will tell you how long it took for that checkout button to load in the first place, and which programs and resources the system utilized along the way.

Underneath user and performance telemetry are different types of signals. A *signal* is a particular form of telemetry. Event logs are one kind of signal. System metrics are another kind of signal. Continuous profiling is another. These signal types each serve a different purpose, and they are not really interchangeable. You can't derive all the events that make up a user interaction just by looking at system metrics, and you can't derive system load just by looking at transaction logs. You need multiple kinds of signals to get a deep understanding of your system as a whole.

Each signal consists of two parts: *instrumentation*—code that emits telemetry data—within the programs themselves, and a *transmission system* for sending the data over the network to an *analysis tool*, where the actual observing occurs.

This raises an important distinction: it's common to conflate telemetry and analysis, but it's important to understand that the system that emits the data and the system that analyzes the data are separate from each other. *Telemetry* is the data itself. *Analysis* is what you do with the data.

Finally, telemetry plus an analysis equals *observability*. Understanding the best way to combine these two pieces into a useful observability system is what this book is all about.

Observability Is a Practice

Observability doesn't stop at the telemetry and analysis; it's an organizational practice, similar to DevOps. In many ways, observability is the foundation of modern software development practices—it underpins everything we do, from continuous integration and deployment to chaos engineering, developer productivity, and more. Your observability sources are as wide and varied as your teams and software, and that data can be collected, analyzed, and used for continuous improvement of your entire organization. We hope you walk away from this book equipped with the foundational knowledge required to establish an observability practice in your organization, built on OpenTelemetry!

A Brief History of Telemetry

Fun fact: it's called *telemetry* because the first remote diagnostic systems transmitted data over telegraph lines. While people often think of rockets and 1950s aerospace when they hear the term *telemetry*, if that was where the practice had started, it would have been called *radiometry*. Telemetry was actually first developed to monitor power plants and public power grids—early but important distributed systems!

Of course, computer telemetry came later. The specific history of user and performance telemetry maps to changes in software operations, and to the ever-increasing processing power and network bandwidth that have long driven those trends. Understanding how computer telemetry signals came to be and how they evolved is an important part of understanding their current limitations.

The first and most enduring form of telemetry was logging. *Logs* are text-based messages meant for human consumption that describe the state of a system or service. Over time, developers and operators improved how they stored and searched these logs by creating specialized databases that were good at full-text search.

While logging did tell you about individual events and moments within a system, understanding how that system was changing over time required more data. A log could tell you that a file couldn't be written because the storage device was out of space, but wouldn't it be great if you could track available storage capacity and make a change *before* you ran out of space?

Metrics are compact statistical representations of system state and resource utilization. They were perfect for the job. Adding metrics made it possible to build alerting on data, beyond errors and exceptions.

As the modern internet took off, systems became more complex, and performance became more critical. A third form of telemetry was added: *distributed tracing*. As transactions grew to include more and more operations and more and more machines, localizing the source of a problem became more critical. Instead of just looking at individual events—logs—tracing systems looked at entire operations and how they combined to form transactions. Operations have a start time and an end time. They also have a location: on which machine did a particular operation occur? Tracking this made it possible to localize the source of latency to a particular operation or a machine. However, because of resource constraints, tracing systems tended to be heavily sampled and ended up recording only a small fraction of the total number of transactions, which limited their usefulness beyond basic performance analysis.

The Three Browser Tabs of Observability

While there are other useful forms of telemetry, the primacy of these three systems—logs, metrics, and tracing—led to the concept known today as the "three pillars of observability."[4] The three pillars are a great way to describe how we currently practice observability—but they're actually a terrible way to *design* a telemetry system!

Traditionally, each form of observability—telemetry plus analysis—was built as a completely separate, siloed system, as described in Figure 1-1.

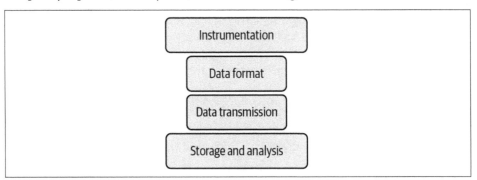

Figure 1-1. A pillar of observability

A logging system consists of logging instrumentation, a log transmission system, and a log analysis tool. A metrics system consists of metrics instrumentation, a metrics transmission system, and a metrics analysis tool. The same is true for tracing—hence the three pillars described in Figure 1-2.

---

4 Cindy Sridharan, *Distributed Systems Observability* (Sebastopol, CA: O'Reilly, 2018).

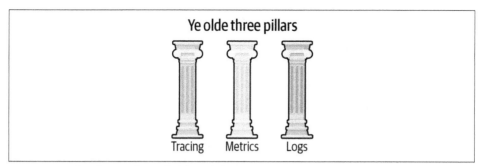

Figure 1-2. The three pillars of observability

This is basic *vertical integration*: each system is built to purpose, end to end. It makes sense that observability has been built this way—it's been evolving over time, with each piece added as it was needed. In other words, observability is structured this way for no better reason than historical accident. The simplest way to implement a logging system or a metrics system is to do it in isolation, as a standalone system.

So, while the term "three pillars" does explain the way traditional observability is architected, it is also problematic—it makes this architecture sound like a good idea! Which it isn't. It's cheeky, but I prefer a different turn of phrase—the "three browser tabs of observability." Because that's what you're actually getting.

Emerging Complications

The problem is that our systems are not composed of logging problems or metrics problems. They are composed of transactions and resources. When a problem occurs, these are the only two things we can modify: developers can change what the transactions do, and operators can change what resources are available. That's it.

But the devil is in the details. It's possible for a simple, isolated bug to be confined to a single transaction. But most production problems emerge from the way many concurrent transactions interact.

A big part of observing real systems involves identifying patterns of bad behavior and then extrapolating to figure out how certain patterns of transactions and resource consumption cause these patterns. That's really difficult to do! It's very hard to predict how transactions and resources will end up interacting in the real world. Tests and small-scale deployments aren't always useful tools for this task, because the problems you are trying to solve do not appear outside of production. These problems are emergent side effects, and they are specific to the way that the physical reality of your production deployment interacts with the system's real users.

This is a pickle! Clearly, your ability to solve these problems depends on the quality of the telemetry your system is emitting in production.

The Three Pillars Were an Accident

You can definitely use metrics, logs, and traces to understand your system. Logs and traces help you reconstruct the events that make up a transaction, while metrics help you understand resource usage and availability.

But useful observations do not come from looking at data in isolation. You can't look at a single data point, or even a single data type, and understand anything about emergent behavior. You'll almost never find the root cause of a problem just by looking at logs or metrics. The clues that lead us to answers come from finding correlations *across* these different data streams. So, when investigating a problem, you tend to pivot back and forth between logs and metrics, looking for correlations.

This is the primary problem with the traditional three pillars approach: these signals are all kept in separate data silos. This makes it impossible to automatically identify correlations between changing patterns in our transaction logs and changing patterns in our metrics. Instead, you end up with three separate browser tabs, and each one contains only a portion of what you need.

Vertical integration makes things even worse: if you want to spot correlations across metrics, logs, and traces, you need these connections to be present in the telemetry your systems are emitting. Without unified telemetry, even if you were able to store these separate signals in the same database, you would still be missing key identifiers that make correlations reliable and consistent. So the three pillars are actually a bad design! What we need is an integrated system.

A Single Braid of Data

How do you triage your systems once you've noticed a problem? By finding correlations. How do you find correlations? There are two ways—with humans and with computers:

Human investigation
> Operators sweep through all the available data, building a mental model of the current system. Then, in their heads, they try to identify how all the pieces might be secretly connected. Not only is this approach mentally exhausting, but it's also subject to the limitations of human memory. Think about it: they're literally looking for correlations by using their *eyeballs* to look at *squiggly lines*. In addition, human investigation suffers as organizations grow larger and systems become more complex. Turning something you see in a squiggly line into an actionable insight becomes harder when the required knowledge is distributed around the world.

Computer investigation

The second way to find correlations is by using computers. Computers may not be good at forming hypotheses and finding root causes, but they are very good at identifying correlations. That's just statistical mathematics.

But again, there's a catch: computers can find correlations only between *connected* pieces of data. And if your telemetry data is siloed, unstructured, and inconsistent, then the assistance computers can offer you will be very limited. This is why human operators are still using their eyeballs to scan for metrics while also trying to memorize every line in every config file.

Instead of three separate pillars, let's use a new metaphor: a single braid of data. Figure 1-3 shows my favorite way of thinking about high-quality telemetry. We still have three separate signals—there's no conflating them—but the signals have touch points that connect everything into a single graphical data structure.

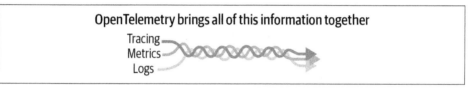

Figure 1-3. A braid of signals, making it easier to find correlations between them

With a telemetry system like this, it's possible for computers to walk through the graph, quickly finding distant but important connections. Unified telemetry means it's finally possible to have unified analysis, which is critical to developing a deep understanding of the emergent problems inherent to live production systems.

Does such a telemetry system exist? It does. And it's called OpenTelemetry.

Conclusion

The world of observability is in the process of changing for the better, and at the heart of that change will be a newfound ability to correlate across all forms of telemetry: traces, metrics, logs, profiling, everything. Correlation is the key to unlocking the workflows and automation that we desperately need to keep up with this world of ever expanding complex systems.

This change is already happening, but it will take some time for the transition to be complete and for observability products to explore the kind of features that this new data unlocks. We are only at the beginning. But since the heart of this transition is a shift to a new kind of data, and since OpenTelemetry is now the widely agreed upon source of that data, understanding OpenTelemetry means understanding the future of observability in general.

This book will be your guide to learning OpenTelemetry. It is not meant to be a replacement for OpenTelemetry documentation, which can be found on the project's website (*https://opentelemetry.io*). Instead, this book explains the philosophy and design of OpenTelemetry and offers practical guidance on how to wield it effectively.

In Chapter 2, we explain the value proposition OpenTelemetry brings, and how your organization benefits from replacing proprietary instrumentation with instrumentation based on open standards.

In Chapter 3, we take a deeper dive into the OpenTelemetry model and discuss the primary observability signals of traces, metrics, and logs, along with how they're linked via context.

In Chapter 4, we get hands-on with OpenTelemetry in the OpenTelemetry Demo, giving you an overview of its components and of how OpenTelemetry fits into an observability stack.

In Chapter 5, we dive into instrumenting an application and provide a checklist to help ensure that everything works and that the telemetry is high-quality.

In Chapter 6, we discuss instrumenting OSS libraries and services and explain why library maintainers should care about observability.

In Chapter 7, we review the options for observing software infrastructure—cloud providers, platforms, and data services.

In Chapter 8, we go into detail on how and why to build different types of observability pipelines using the OpenTelemetry Collector.

In Chapter 9, we provide advice on how to deploy OpenTelemetry across your organization. Since telemetry—especially tracing—is a cross-team issue, there are organizational pitfalls when rolling out a new observability system. This chapter will provide strategies and advice on how to ensure a successful rollout.

Finally, our appendices include helpful resources on the structure of the OpenTelemetry project itself, as well as links to further reading and other titles.

If you are brand new to OpenTelemetry, we strongly suggest reading up through Chapter 4 first. After that, the chapters can be read in any order. Feel free to skip to whichever section is most relevant to the task you need to accomplish.

CHAPTER 2

Why Use OpenTelemetry?

A map is not the actual territory.
—Alfred Korzybski[1]

If you're reading this, you're almost certainly in the business of software. Your job may be to solve business or human problems by writing code, or to ensure that great fleets of software and servers are highly available and responsive to requests. Or maybe that *was* your job at one point and now you tackle technical problems of a different sort—how to organize, coordinate, and motivate human beings to efficiently ship and maintain software.

Software itself is a vital part of our global economy; the only things more crucial are the people tasked with its creation and upkeep. And the scale of their task is enormous—modern developers and operations teams are being asked to do more with less, even as system complexity grows without bounds. You get some documentation, a group of like-minded individuals, and 40 hours a week to keep systems running that generate measurable fractions of the global gross domestic product.

It doesn't take too long to realize that this is, perhaps, not quite enough.

The map of your software system that you build in your mind will inevitably drift away from that on paper. Your understanding of what's happening at any given time is always limited by how expansive the system is, how many changes are occurring in it, and how many people are changing it. New innovations, such as generative AI, bring this observation into sharp focus—these components are true black boxes, where you have little to no insight into *how* they come to their results.

---

1 Alfred Korzybski, "A Non-Aristotelian System and Its Necessity for Rigour in Mathematics and Physics" (paper, presented at annual meeting of the American Association for the Advancement of Science, New Orleans, Louisiana, December 28, 1931), *https://oreil.ly/YnvRH*.

Telemetry and observability are your most potent weapons to combat this drift. As we discussed in Chapter 1, telemetry data tells you what your system is doing. However, the status quo of telemetry is not a sustainable one. OpenTelemetry seeks to upend this status quo, delivering not just *more* data but *better* data, data that serves the needs of the people who build and run systems and the organizations and businesses powered by those systems.

Production Monitoring: The Status Quo

Imagine for a moment that you don't work in software at all. Your job is to manage the public-transit system of a growing municipality.

Your transit system started out small—just a handful of buses that operated on a fairly fixed schedule. This was fine until more people moved in and started demanding more service to more places. More business and industry came in, and suddenly the local government is mandating that you build specific one-off lines to remote industrial parks and light-rail service between outlying areas.

Think about everything you might want to monitor in this scenario. You would want to know how many vehicles you have in service, certainly, and where they are at any given point in time. You would want to know how many people are riding transit, in order to more efficiently allocate limited resources. You would also want to know about the maintenance status of your fleet so you can predict wear and tear, and possibly avoid emergency repairs. Different stakeholders will want to know different things as well, at different levels of detail. The city council probably doesn't need to know about the tire-tread levels of every bus, but your maintenance supervisor certainly does—and you might too, in order to plan capital expenses.

This is a lot of data! It's an overwhelming amount of data, in fact. And the worst part is, it's not *consistent*. Your maintenance data relies on humans to transcribe and report values accurately. Your ridership data relies on sensors or ticket counts. Vehicle statistics come in all different types—and different vehicles in your fleet may report the same thing in different ways. How do you standardize this data? How do you analyze it? How do you ensure that you're collecting what you need to, and how do you make changes to which data you collect over time?

This hypothetical should sound somewhat familiar to anyone who's been building software for a while. All production software systems are a combination of decisions built up over time, and much of the work of operating them involves collecting, normalizing, interpreting, and parceling out data to various stakeholders for various purposes. Developers need highly detailed telemetry that they can use to pinpoint specific problems in code. Operators need broad, aggregated information from across hundreds or thousands of servers and nodes so that they can spot trends and respond quickly to outliers. Security teams need to analyze many millions of events across endpoints to discover potential intrusions; business analysts need to understand how customers interact with features and how performance impacts customer experience; directors and leaders need to understand the overall health of the system in order to prioritize work and expenditures.

The current status quo of production monitoring is that we use dozens of tools to collect a variety of signals in different formats on varying cadences, and then we send them off for storage and analysis. Smaller organizations may be able to put everything into a single database or data lake; larger organizations may find themselves with hundreds of storage destinations that have a variety of access controls. As organizational complexity increases, analyzing and responding to incidents becomes more difficult. Outages take longer to detect, diagnose, and remediate because the people doing that work don't have the right data at hand.

The Challenges of Production Debugging

Most organizations face three main challenges when trying to understand their software systems: the amount of data that they need to parse, the quality of that data, and how the data fits together.

These problems have similar factors in common. There are no universal standards for creating telemetry. Telemetry signals are independently generated. There will be technical and organizational impediments to creating quality telemetry, and existing systems have their own momentum. The results are clear: incidents take longer to detect and remediate,[2] software engineers burn out faster,[3] and software quality drops. Anecdotally, we've heard stories from (very large) organizations of incidents that stretch into days or weeks because of the difficulty of sharing data among incident responders. In many organizations, it's not uncommon to have to navigate between multiple independent monitoring tools in order to discover why a particular API is slow or why a customer is experiencing errors uploading a file. The cloud, and especially Kubernetes, makes this task even more challenging, since containers are created and destroyed at will by the cluster, taking uncollected logs with them.

Complicating this further, many debugging techniques are difficult to use when your systems are changing rapidly. The nodes on which your workload runs may change from hour to hour, or even minute to minute, in cloud environments. Discovering a

---

2 The VOID Report for 2022 (*https://oreil.ly/xuh5c*) includes many interesting insights into the lack of a relationship between incident severity and duration, leading us to conclude that the important thing in telemetry isn't its utility in reducing mean time to respond (MTTR).

3 Tien Rahayu Tulili, Andrea Capiluppi, and Ayushi Rastogi, "Burnout in software engineering: A systematic mapping study," *Information and Software Technology* 155, (March 2023): 107116, *https://oreil.ly/d9AMZ* This review of studies about burnout in software development and IT found that "work exhaustion" was one of the most significant and durable predictors of turnover.

slow node, network misconfigurations, or code that performs poorly under specific circumstances is extremely challenging when "where the code is running" can change in the middle of observing a failure.

To address this problem, system operators employ a wide array of tools, such as log parsers, metric-collection rules, and other complex telemetry pipelines, to collect, store, and normalize telemetry data for their use. Many businesses use proprietary tooling that collects this data in a massive managed platform, but this comes with its own trade-offs. The cost of managed platforms can be extremely high, and unless you want to go through an expensive migration process, you're stuck with the features of that platform. If no one platform solves all your problems, you may be stuck managing multiple platforms, or a combination of platforms and point solutions, for specific features and functionality (such as frontend or mobile client observability). Organizations that build their own platforms wind up having to "reinvent the wheel" by creating their own instrumentation, collection, storage, and visualization layers at great expense.

How can the industry overcome these challenges? Our philosophy is that these challenges stem from a lack of high-quality, standards-based, consistent telemetry data. If observability is to make a difference in developers' lives, then, as Charity Majors and her coauthors write, it "requires evolving the way we think about gathering the data needed to debug effectively."[4]

The Importance of Telemetry

To solve the challenges of production monitoring and debugging, you need to rethink your approach to telemetry data. Rather than the three pillars of metrics, logs, and traces we mentioned in Chapter 1, you need an interwoven braid.

What does this mean in practice, though? In this section, you'll learn about the three characteristics of unifying telemetry that OpenTelemetry practices: hard and soft context, telemetry layering, and semantic telemetry.

Hard and Soft Context

Context is an overloaded term in the monitoring and observability space. It can refer to a very literal object in your application, to data being passed over an RPC link, or to the logical and linguistic meaning of the term. However, the actual meaning is fairly consistent between these definitions: context is metadata that helps describe the relationship between system operations and telemetry.

---

4 Charity Majors, Liz Fong-Jones, and George Miranda, *Observability Engineering* (Sebastopol, CA: O'Reilly, 2022), 8.

Broadly speaking, there are two types of context that you care about, and those contexts appear in two places. The types of context are what we'll refer to as "hard" and "soft" contexts, and they appear in an application or in infrastructure. An observability frontend can identify and support varying mixtures of these contexts, but without them, the value of telemetry data is significantly reduced—or vanishes altogether.

A *hard context* is a unique, per-request identifier that services in a distributed application can propagate to other services that are part of the same request. A basic model of this would be a single request from a web client through a load balancer into an API server, which calls a function in another service to read a database and returns some computed value to the client (see Figure 2-1). This can also be referred to as the *logical context* of the request (as it maps to a single desired end-user interaction with the system).

A *soft context* would be various pieces of metadata that each telemetry instrument attaches to measurements from the various services and infrastructure that handle that same request—for example, a customer identifier, the hostname of the load balancer that served the request, or the timestamp of a piece of telemetry data (also pictured in Figure 2-1). The key distinction between hard and soft contexts is that a hard context directly and explicitly links measurements that have a causal relationship, whereas soft contexts *may* do so but are not *guaranteed* to.

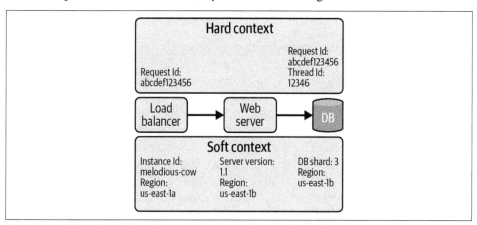

Figure 2-1. "Hard" and "soft" contexts emitted by a web application

Without contexts, the value of telemetry is significantly reduced, because you lose the ability to associate measurements with each other. The more context you add, the easier it becomes to interrogate your data for useful insights, especially as you add more concurrent transactions to a distributed system.

In a system with low levels of concurrency, soft contexts may be suitable for explaining system behavior. As complexity and concurrency increase, however, a human operator will quickly be overwhelmed by data points, and the value of the telemetry will drop to zero. You can see the value of soft context in Figure 2-2, where viewing the average latency of a particular endpoint doesn't give a lot of helpful clues as to any underlying problems, but adding context (a customer attribute) allows you to quickly identify a user-facing problem.

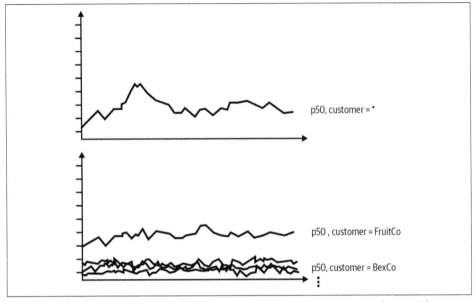

Figure 2-2. A time-series metric showing average latency for an API endpoint. The top graph plots average (p50) latency; the bottom graph applies a single group-by context. You can see that the overall average is higher because of a single outlier, FruitCo.

The soft context most commonly used in monitoring is time. One tried-and-true method of spotting differences or correlating cause and effect is to align multiple time windows across several different instruments or data sources and then visually interpret the output. Again, as complexity increases, this method becomes less effective. Traditionally, operators are forced to layer in additional soft contexts, "zooming in and out" until they've identified a sufficiently narrow lens through which they can actually find useful results in their data set.

Hard context, on the other hand, can dramatically simplify this exploratory process. A hard context not only allows the association of individual telemetry measurements with other measurements of the same type—for example, ensuring that individual spans within a trace are linked together—but also enables *linking different types of instruments*. For example, you can associate metrics with traces, link logs to spans, and so forth. The presence of hard context can dramatically reduce the time a human operator spends investigating anomalous behavior in a system. Hard context is also useful for building certain visualizations, such as a *service map*, or a diagram of the relationships in a system. You can see this in Figure 2-3, where each service in a system is visually linked to the other services that it communicates with. Identifying these relationships *just* with soft context is difficult and usually requires human intervention.

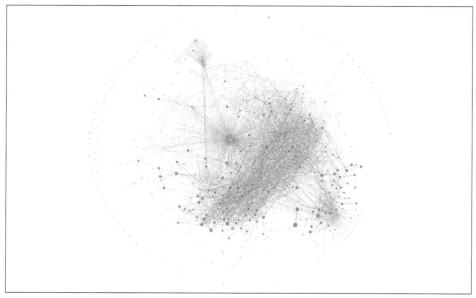

Figure 2-3. A large microservice system map, from Uber.[5] This kind of diagram is made possible using the hard context provided by distributed tracing.

To summarize: *Hard context* defines the overall shape of a system by defining relationships between services and signals. *Soft context* allows you to create unique dimensions across telemetry signals that help explain what a particular signal represents.

We'll get to the "how" later in the book, but OpenTelemetry is designed from the ground up to provide both hard and soft context to all signals it emits. For now, keep in mind that these contexts are crucial to creating unified telemetry.

Telemetry Layering

Telemetry signals are generally convertible. As an example, content delivery networks (CDNs) such as Cloudflare give you dashboards full of website performance metrics, showing you the rate of requests broken down by HTTP status code. The underlying data for this is log statements, parsed into time-series metrics.

---

5 "Introducing Domain-Oriented Microservice Architecture," *Uber Blog*, July 23, 2020, *https://oreil.ly/FNb43*. This screenshot (taken in mid-2018) shows services and their relationships.

This is a fairly common practice for most monitoring and observability tools, but it has drawbacks. Costs are associated with these conversions, both in resources (they take CPU and memory) and in time (the more you convert and transform a piece of data, the longer it takes before the resulting measurement is available). There's also a time cost to managing and maintaining transformation and parsing rules. This is toil, plain and simple, and it makes it difficult to understand what's happening in production. Often, a system can fail for users for many minutes before alerts start to fire—and that's because the system is using telemetry signals inefficiently.

A better solution is to *layer* telemetry signals and use them in complementary ways, rather than attempting to turn a single "dense" signal, such as application logs, into other forms. You can use more tailored instruments to measure application and system behavior at specific layers of abstraction, link those signals through contexts, and layer your telemetry to get the *right* data from these overlapping signals. You can then record and store it in appropriate, efficient ways. Such data can answer questions about your system that you might not even have known you had. Layering telemetry, as shown in Figure 2-4, allows you to better understand and model your systems.

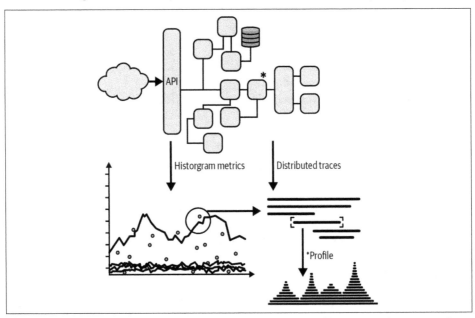

Figure 2-4. An illustration of layered signals. A histogram measures API latency, with exemplars linking to specific traces, and with those traces linking to profiles or logs to get component- or function-level insights.

OpenTelemetry is built with this concept in mind. Signals are linked to each other through hard context—for example, metrics can have *exemplars* appended to them that link a specific measurement to a given trace. Logs also are attached to trace contexts as they're processed. This means you can make better decisions about what type of data to emit and store based on factors such as throughput, alert thresholds, and service level objectives and agreements.

Semantic Telemetry

Monitoring is a passive action. Observability is an active practice. To analyze the territory of a system—to understand how it actually works and performs in production, rather than relying on the parts you can see, like code or documentation—you need more than just passive dashboards and alerts based on telemetry data.

Even highly contextual and layered telemetry is not enough by itself to achieve observability. You need to store that data somewhere, and you need to actively analyze it. Your ability to effectively consume telemetry is thus limited by many factors—storage, network bandwidth, telemetry creation overhead (how much memory or CPU is utilized to actually create and transmit signals), analysis cost, alert evaluation rate, and much more. To be more blunt, your ability to understand a software system is ultimately a cost-optimization exercise. How much are you willing to spend in order to understand your system?

This fact causes significant pain for existing monitoring practices. Developers are often restricted on the amount of context they can provide, as the amount of metadata attached to telemetry increases the cost of storing and querying that telemetry. In addition, different signals will often be analyzed multiple times for distinct purposes. As an example, HTTP access logs are a good source of data for the performance of a given server. They are also critical information for security teams keeping an eye out for unauthorized access or usage of production systems. This means that the data must be processed multiple times, by multiple tools, for multiple ends.

As we mentioned earlier in this chapter, the result is that developers are usually spelunking through multiple tools with different interfaces and query semantics, dealing with differing representations of the same data, hoping that what they need didn't get thrown away for being too expensive to store.

OpenTelemetry seeks to change this through portable, semantic telemetry: *portable*, as in you can use it with any observability frontend, and *semantic*, as in self-describing. For example, a metric point in OpenTelemetry contains metadata that tells a frontend the granularity of the metric, as well as a description of each unique attribute. The frontend can use this to better visualize metric queries and allow you to search not just for the name of a measurement but for what it's actually measuring.

Fundamentally, OpenTelemetry is an evolutionary step in understanding systems. It is in many ways a summation of the past two decades of work in defining and unifying observability as a concept. As an industry, we've been innovating faster than we can implement or define meaningful standards. OpenTelemetry changes that calculus. With that in mind, let's talk about the problems that OpenTelemetry solves for developers, operators, and organizations.

What Do People Need?

Telemetry and observability have many stakeholders. Different groups and individuals will have different requirements for an observability system, and it stands to reason that they will also have different requirements for telemetry data itself. How can OpenTelemetry satisfy these broad and often competing interests?

In this section, we'll discuss the benefits of OpenTelemetry for developers and operators as well as for teams and organizations.

Developers and Operators

The people who build and operate software need their observability data to be high in quality, highly contextual, highly correlated, and layered, among other things. They need telemetry to be built-in, not something they have to add in later. They need it to be consistently ubiquitous (available from many sources). And they need to be able to modify it—both by changing built-in telemetry and by adding new telemetry—in a consistent fashion across many languages, runtimes, clouds, and so on.

Today, developers use instrumentation libraries to create this data, and they have many existing options, such as Log4j, StatsD, Prometheus, and Zipkin. Proprietary tools also offer their own instrumentation APIs and software development kits (SDKs), along with built-in integrations for popular frameworks, libraries, databases, and so forth.

Ultimately, these instrumentation libraries and formats matter a lot to developers and operators because they define how—and how well—you can model your system through telemetry. The choice of instrumentation library can limit the effective observability of your system: if you can't emit the right signals, with the right context and semantics, you may find yourself simply unable to answer certain questions. One of the biggest challenges that developers face as they learn observability is that everyone does it a *little* differently than everyone else. Organizations with strong, centralized platform engineering and internal tooling teams may offer powerful, well-integrated instrumentation libraries and telemetry, but many do not.

One of the motivating problems for observability is that systems are too large and complex for people to hold them in their heads and understand. Certainly, there have always been large and complex software systems, but what's really different now is the rate of change and the resulting loss of human understanding. In a slower-paced world, there were people who understood the nuances of an application and how it all fit together—we called them *quality assurance (QA)*. Over time, as more organizations jettison traditional QA processes and replace them with continuous integration and delivery, it's become harder for people to absorb the "shape" of a system. The faster we go, the more we need ubiquitous, high-quality telemetry that describes what's happening and why.

Beyond instrumentation libraries and high-quality telemetry, operators need a rich ecosystem of tools to help them collect and process telemetry data. When you generate petabytes of logs, metrics, and traces every day, you need a way to cut through the noise so you can find the signal, which is no small order! There's simply too much data to store and look through later, and most of that data is probably not very interesting. Thus, operators rely on instrumentation that can produce a wide range of signals, as well as tools to help them filter out the things that don't matter so that they can, together with developers, ensure system reliability and resilience.

Teams and Organizations

Observability isn't just for developers. Its stakeholders also include security analysts, project managers, and the C-suite. They may need different views of the same data, at a different resolution, but observability is still a crucial part of any organization's threat posture, business planning, and overall health.

You can think of these as the needs of "the business," but they're more than that. Everyone benefits from the following:

- Open standards that prevent vendor lock-in
- Standard data formats and wire protocols
- Composable, extensible, and well-documented instrumentation libraries and tools

Predictability is catnip to most organizations—that's why processes exist! They trade efficiency for reducing risk (most businesses' least favorite word). It's fine to take risks with innovative practices; it's less fine to take risks around knowing whether your application is up and running. Thus, standards are the order of the day for organizations and their observability needs.

Standards-based approaches have many benefits. *Maintainability* is one example—adopting an open format means that developers and teams have increased training opportunities. Rather than new engineers slowly being onboarded to your custom in-house solution, they can build knowledge on how to instrument using an open standard and carry that with them. This improves your ability to maintain existing instrumentation as well as to onboard new developers as productive members of the team.

Open standards aren't just less risky; they're future-proof. Look around—between 2021 and 2023, the industry saw multiple rounds of consolidation, buyouts, and failures of observability products large and small. Over the past 20 years we've seen multiple metric formats be created and popularized, only to plateau or be diminished by new entrants.

Beyond being simply "nice to have," open standards and open source are essential as you evaluate and build your observability practice. You don't have to look too far to see some of the drawbacks associated with going all-in on proprietary solutions—Coinbase spent $65 million on Datadog (*https://oreil.ly/606GK*) in 2022! We're not saying it wasn't worth it, but gosh, that's a *lot* of money.

The last important factor for organizations is compatibility. It's unlikely that you'd rip out your existing (functional) instrumentation just to switch to something new, and in most cases doing so would be unwise, unless you're getting significantly more value. There aren't many hard-and-fast rules about this, so what you need is the ability to bridge old and new, to adopt new practices while maintaining what you already have in place, and to "level up" your existing telemetry into standard formats.

Why Use OpenTelemetry?

Given all of the requirements of these many stakeholders, what makes OpenTelemetry an ideal solution? At the highest level, OpenTelemetry provides two fundamental values that cannot be found elsewhere.

Universal Standards

OpenTelemetry solves the problems inherent to the status quo in observability. It provides a way to create high-quality, ubiquitous telemetry. It offers a standard way to represent and transmit that telemetry to any observability frontend, eliminating vendor lock-in. It seeks to make telemetry a built-in feature of cloud native software, and in many ways it is accomplishing this goal. As of this writing, all three major cloud providers (Amazon, Azure, and Google Cloud Platform) support OpenTelemetry and are moving to standardize on it. All major observability platforms and tools accept OpenTelemetry data in some way. More and more libraries and frameworks are adopting OpenTelemetry every month.

OpenTelemetry presages a future in which telemetry is truly a commodity and works to make that future a reality. The future it builds is one in which all software creates a rich stream of telemetry data, just below the surface, that you can tap into and pick what you need based on your observability goals. It's more than just an emerging standard—it's inevitable at this point, and it's something you will need to adopt.

Correlated Data

OpenTelemetry is not just a codification of prior practices. To push the field forward, the next generation of observability tools needs to effectively model the workflows that operators perform when investigating their systems. They also need to employ machine learning to surface correlations that might otherwise be difficult to intuit.

Smooth workflows and high-quality correlations can happen only when all of the telemetry is regularized and interconnected. OpenTelemetry is not just a pile of traces, metrics, and logs dumped together in the same place. All these pieces are part of the same data structure, connected together into a single graph that describes the entire system over time.

Conclusion

In this chapter, we've discussed the challenges of production monitoring and the needs of developers, organizations, and observability tools vis-à-vis telemetry data. This is the motivating rationale for why you should use OpenTelemetry.

Now that we've discussed *why*, the rest of this book will address *how* you can successfully adopt OpenTelemetry. We'll start by giving you a tour and an overview of OpenTelemetry's code and components, and then we'll dive deeper into the three primary observability signals (traces, metrics, and logs) and talk about OpenTelemetry's data format in more detail.

CHAPTER 3

OpenTelemetry Overview

You can't communicate complexity, only an awareness of it.
   —Alan J. Perlis[1]

OpenTelemetry contains everything you need to create a modern telemetry system. To understand it, you need to know how it fits into the landscape of not only cloud native software but also the greater commercial and open source observability market.

OpenTelemetry solves two big problems. First, it gives developers a single solution for built-in, native instrumentation of their code. Second, it allows for instrumentation and telemetry data to be broadly compatible with the rest of the observability ecosystem.

These problems have enough in common that they're effectively the same challenge, but it's good to clarify exactly what we mean by breaking them apart. *Built-in (or native) instrumentation* in this context means that a library, service, managed system, or something similar is creating a variety of telemetry signals directly from the application code that are linked with other signals.

You need to be able to create and process data using not just a common API or SDK but a set of "nouns and verbs"—a common set of definitions around what things mean (also known as *semantics)*. This isn't just about having consistent attributes across signals, although that's part of it. You need consistent attributes and labels across your telemetry in order to correlate it together. Truly native instrumentation is about having *semantically accurate* instrumentation.

---

1 Alan J. Perlis, "Epigrams on Programming," *SIGPLAN Notices* 17, no. 9 (September 1982): 7–13.

To learn OpenTelemetry, you need to know more than just how to create a span or initialize the SDK—you need to understand the signals, the context, and the conventions, and how they all fit together. We'll get into the finer details in Chapters 5 through 8, but let's start by understanding the model OpenTelemetry uses to fit all these pieces together. Figure 3-1 shows this model at the highest level.

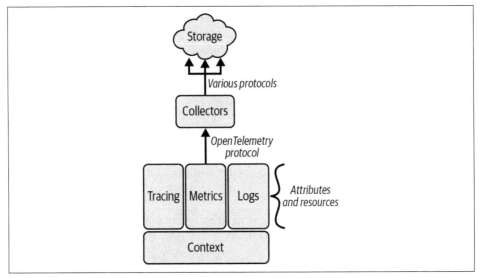

Figure 3-1. A high-level model of OpenTelemetry

In the rest of this chapter, we'll dive into each component of this model. We'll start with the types of signals that OpenTelemetry produces, the context that binds these signals together, and the attributes and conventions used to model different types of libraries and software components. Then we'll have a look at the protocols and services used to create a pipeline to send all of these signals to an observability tool for storage and analysis. At the end, we'll briefly touch on OpenTelemetry's commitment to stability and future-proofing.

Primary Observability Signals

As alluded to in Chapter 1, *instrumentation* is the process of adding observability code to a service or system. Broadly, there are two ways to perform this. The first is through a "white-box" approach that involves directly adding telemetry code to a service or library, and the second is a "black-box" approach that utilizes external agents or libraries to generate telemetry without requiring direct code changes. In both cases, your objective is to generate one or more *signals*—raw data about what's happening in a process. OpenTelemetry concerns itself with three primary signals:

traces, metrics, and logs.[2] These signals are ordered roughly by importance. Their importance comes from the following goals:

- Capturing the relationships between services in your system using actual production data and service-to-service communication
- Annotating service telemetry with consistent and descriptive metadata about what the service is doing and where it's running
- Definitively identifying the relationships between arbitrary groups of measurements—basically, "this thing happened at the same time as this other thing"
- Efficiently creating accurate counts and measurements of events occurring in a system, such as the number of requests that occur, or how many requests took between 100 and 150 milliseconds to complete

These tasks can be fiendishly difficult at scale; the amount of money large enterprises spend on performing even simple tasks, such as enumerating the amount and criticality of various services, is staggering. Smaller organizations are beginning to suffer similar challenges, as the complexity of cloud native architectures results in a significant amount of ephemeral and dynamic work being performed. OpenTelemetry is designed to provide the building blocks needed to answer these questions, and perform these tasks, for cloud native architectures. Thus, OpenTelemetry focuses on providing semantically accurate instrumentation for cloud native software.

Let's discuss each of the three primary signals in turn.

Traces

A *trace* is a way to model work in a distributed system. You can think of it as a set of log statements that follow a well-defined schema. The work done by each service in the system is linked together through hard context, as shown in Figure 3-2. Tracing is the fundamental signal of observability for a distributed system. Each trace is a collection of related logs, called *spans*, for a given transaction. Each span in turn contains a variety of fields.[3] If you're familiar with structured logging, you can think of a trace as a set of logs that are correlated through a shared identifier.

---

2 OpenTelemetry is currently working to add support for sessions and profiles; a *session* is a signal used to represent a continuous client session in a web or mobile client, while a *profile* is a set of stack traces and metrics used for line-level performance data.

3 See the OpenTelemetry Specifications (*https://opentelemetry.io/docs/specs*) for a full dissection of these fields and their purposes.

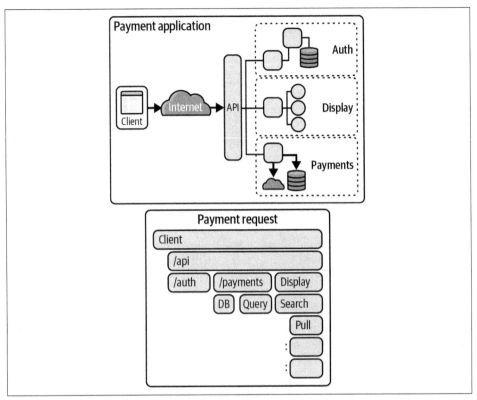

Figure 3-2. A basic payment application for a store. The trace underneath describes a payment request

The difference between structured logs and tracing, though, is that tracing is an incredibly powerful observability signal for request/response transactions, which are prevalent throughout cloud native distributed systems. Traces offer several semantic benefits that make them a valuable observability signal—for example:

- A single trace represents a single transaction, or journey, through a distributed system. This makes traces the best way to model end-user experience, since one trace corresponds to one user's path through a system.

- A group of traces can be aggregated across multiple dimensions in order to discover performance characteristics that would be difficult to spot otherwise.

- Traces can be transformed into other signals, such as metrics, allowing for down-sampling of the raw data without losing key performance information. In other words, a single trace contains all the information needed to compute the "golden signals" (latency, traffic, errors, and saturation) for a single request.

Golden Signals

The golden signals are the four crucial measurements you should take of a system, as defined in the Google SRE Handbook (*https://oreil.ly/aw2iQ*). *Latency* is the time it takes to service a request, *traffic* is the number of requests, *errors* represent the rate of failing requests, and *saturation* is a measure of utilization of system resources.

Tracing is the core of transaction observability. It is the best way to understand the performance, health, and behavior of a distributed system in production. It's not the only way to measure a system, though, and observability requires you to blend multiple signals together. With that in mind, let's discuss one of the most widespread signals: metrics.

Metrics

Metrics are numeric measurements and recordings of system state, such as the number of users concurrently logged into a system, the amount of disk space used on a device, or the amount of RAM available on a virtual machine (VM). They're useful for accurately measuring the "big picture" of a system because they're cheap to create and store.

Metrics are often the first port of call for developers trying to understand overall system health. They're ubiquitous, fast, and inexpensive for what they do. There are some challenges with traditional metrics, though. Traditionally, they lack hard context—it's difficult, and in some cases impossible, to accurately correlate a given metric with specific end-user transactions. They can also be difficult to modify, especially when they're defined in third-party libraries and frameworks. This raises challenges when two similar metrics are inconsistent in how, or when, they report things. We know from speaking with operators and observability teams that controlling the costs and complexity of metrics is one of their primary challenges.

In OpenTelemetry, metrics have been designed to support three main goals:

- Developers should be able to define important, semantically meaningful events in their code and specify how those events translate into metric signals.
- Operators should be able to control costs, data volume, and resolution by aggregating or reaggregating the time or attributes of those metrics.
- Conversions should not change the intrinsic meaning of a measurement.

By way of example, imagine you want to measure the size of incoming requests through a service that processes images. OpenTelemetry allows you to record this size in bytes through a metric instrument and then apply aggregations to those events, such as determining the maximum size recorded over a time window, or adding them together to get the total number of bytes for a given attribute. These streams are then exported to other OpenTelemetry components, where they can be further modified—by adding or removing attributes, for example, or by modifying the time window—without altering the meaning of the measurements.

This may seem like a lot to absorb, but here are the important takeaways:

- OpenTelemetry metrics include semantic meaning that observability pipelines or frontends can take advantage of to intelligently query and visualize metric streams.
- OpenTelemetry metrics can be linked to other signals through both hard and soft context, allowing you to layer telemetry signals for cost control or other purposes.
- OpenTelemetry metrics support StatsD and Prometheus out of the box, allowing you to map those existing metrics signals into the OpenTelemetry ecosystem.

Exemplars

OpenTelemetry metrics have a special type of hard context known as *exemplars*, which allow you to link an event to a specific span and trace. In Chapter 5, we'll discuss how to create these metrics and use them in your applications.

Logs

Logging is the final primary signal, and perhaps it's surprising to you that we'd cover it last. After all, logs are ubiquitous for their ease of use—they're the lowest common denominator of methods to get the computer to tell you what it's doing. OpenTelemetry's log support has more to do with supporting the existing logging APIs that you're comfortable and familiar with, rather than trying to reinvent the wheel.

That said, existing logging solutions are weakly coupled to other observability signals. Associating log data with traces or metrics is usually accomplished through correlations. These correlations are performed either by aligning time windows (such as "what happened between 09:30:25 and 09:31:07") or by comparing shared attributes. There's not a standard way to include uniform metadata, or to link log signals with traces and metrics, in order to discover causal relationships. Distributed systems, such as those common in cloud native architectures, often wind up with highly disjointed sets of logs that are collected from different components in the system and often centralized in different tools.

Fundamentally, the OpenTelemetry model seeks to unify this signal by enriching log statements with trace context and links to metrics and traces recorded concomitantly. In plainer terms, OpenTelemetry can take existing log statements in your application code, see if there's an existing context, and, if so, ensure that the log statements are associated with that context.

Some readers may ask about the role of logs in observability, and it's a fair question. Traditionally, logging occupies the same "mental space" as tracing in terms of utility, but logs are perceived as being more flexible and easier to use. In OpenTelemetry, there are four main reasons to use logs:

- To get signals out of services that can't be traced, such as legacy code, mainframes, and other systems of record
- To correlate infrastructure resources such as managed databases or load balancers with application events
- To understand behavior in a system that isn't tied to a user request, such as cron jobs or other recurring and on-demand work
- To process them into other signals, such as metrics or traces

Again, we'll go into more depth about how to create and set up log pipelines in later chapters. Next, though, we'll delve more deeply into how each signal in OpenTelemetry can be linked via hard and soft context, and we'll introduce you to the specifics of observability context.

Observability Context

We introduced several ideas in the prior section—*attributes*, *resources*, and so forth. They're all, on some level, the same thing—metadata. Understanding the differences and similarities between them, however, is a crucial part of learning OpenTelemetry. Logically, they're all forms of context.

If a signal gives you some sort of measurement or data point, the context is what makes that data relevant. Think back to our earlier example of a transit planner. Knowing how many people across the entire city are waiting for a bus is useful, but it would be impossible to understand where you need to add more buses without the *context* of where those people are waiting.

There are three basic types of context in OpenTelemetry: time, attributes, and the context object itself. Time is fairly self-explanatory: when did something happen? We'll discuss the rest next.

OK, but When DID Something Happen?

Time seems like a very logical way to order events, but it's incredibly unreliable when thinking about telemetry in a distributed system. Clocks can drift and become inaccurate because of a variety of factors, including paused execution of a thread, resource exhaustion, device sleep/wake behavior, or loss of network connectivity. Even in a single JavaScript process, the system clock can lose up to ~100ms of precision over the course of a single hour. This is one of many reasons that specific contexts—such as the relationship between calls in a trace, or shared attributes—are so useful.

The Context Layer

As mentioned earlier, context is an essential part of a telemetry system. The Open-Telemetry Context Specification (*https://oreil.ly/XXX4L*) seems deceptively simple from this perspective. At a high level, the specification defines *context* as a "propagation mechanism which carries execution-scoped values across API boundaries and between logically associated execution units." (An *execution unit* (*https://oreil.ly/2TvZA*) is a thread, coroutine, or other sequential code execution construct in a language.) In other words, contexts carry information across a gap: between two services running on the same computer through a pipe, between different servers through remote procedure calls, or between different threads in a single process (Figure 3-3).

The goal of the context layer is to provide a clean interface either to existing context managers (such as Golang's context.Context, Java ThreadLocals, or Python's context manager) or to some other suitable carrier. What's important is that the context is required and that it holds one or more propagators.

Propagators (*https://oreil.ly/zYaig*) are how you actually send values from one process to the next. When a request begins, OpenTelemetry creates a unique identifier for that request based on registered propagators. This identifier can then be added to the context, serialized, and sent to the next service, which will deserialize it and add it to the local context.[4]

---

4 OpenTelemetry uses W3C Trace Context (*https://www.w3.org/TR/trace-context*) as a default propagator across RPCs and other services, but it supports other options, such as B3 Trace Context and AWS X-Ray.

Baggage

Propagators carry the hard context of a request (such as W3C Trace Context), but they can also carry what's known as *baggage*, or *soft-context values*. Baggage is meant to transmit certain values that you may wish to put on other signals (for example, customer or session IDs) from where they were created to other parts of your system. Once baggage is added, it cannot be removed and will be transmitted to external systems as well—so be careful about what you put in there!

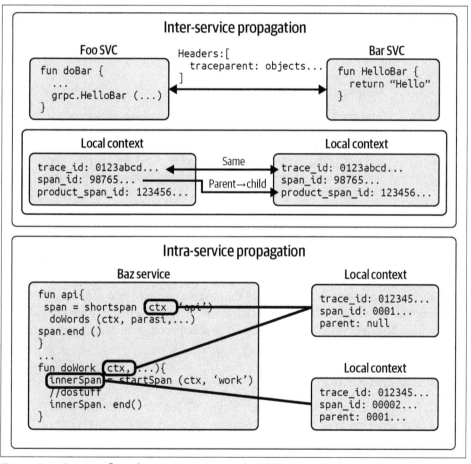

Figure 3-3. Context flows between services and within a service (inter-service versus intra-service propagation)

This forms the basis of hard context in OpenTelemetry: any service with OpenTelemetry tracing enabled will create and use tracing contexts to create telemetry data representing the work being done in that service. In addition, OpenTelemetry can associate this context with other telemetry signals such as metrics or logs.

This isn't the only type of context OpenTelemetry is able to provide, however. The project maintains a variety of semantic conventions (*https://oreil.ly/lmRoT*) to create a consistent and clear set of metadata that can be applied to telemetry signals. These conventions allow for analysis across standard dimensions, reducing the need for data to be postprocessed and normalized. These semantics run the gamut from metadata (to represent resources such as server hostnames, IP addresses, or cloud regions) to specific naming conventions for HTTP routes, serverless execution environment information, and pub-sub messaging queue directions. You can find an example (*https://oreil.ly/otelex*) on the OpenTelemetry project site.

Merging standards

In April 2023, OpenTelemetry and Elastic announced the merger (*https://oreil.ly/Q_EAi*) of the Elastic Common Schema with OpenTelemetry Semantic Conventions. This process will result in fewer competing standards for telemetry metadata once it's complete and is a great example of the value of standards-making efforts in the cloud native space.

The goal of the semantic conventions process is to create a standardized and representative set of metadata that can accurately model and describe the underlying resources that power not only a given transaction in a distributed system but also *the actual transaction itself*. Think back to earlier in this chapter where we discussed semantic instrumentation. If the traces, metrics, and logs are the verbs that describe how your system functions, the semantic conventions provide the nouns that describe what it's doing. We'll go deeper into this topic in "Semantic Conventions" on page 37.

Attributes and Resources

Every piece of telemetry that's emitted by OpenTelemetry has attributes. You may have heard these referred to as *fields* or *tags* in other monitoring systems. These attributes are a form of metadata that tell you what a piece of telemetry represents. Simply put, an *attribute* is a key-value pair that describes an interesting, or useful, dimension of a piece of telemetry. Attributes are things you'd want to filter on or group by if you were trying to understand what's happening in your system.

Let's go back to our transit system. If you wanted to measure how many people are using it, you'd have a single quantity—the count of riders in a given day. Attributes give that measurement useful dimensions, such as the form of transit someone is using, the station they departed from, or even unique identifiers such as their name. With those attributes, you can ask some really interesting questions that you couldn't ask if all you knew were how many people were riding! You can see which modes of transit were most popular or whether particular stations were overloaded. With highly unique attributes, you could even track ridership across time to see if there were interesting patterns of use.

Similarly, when you are asking questions about a distributed system, you might want to consider a variety of dimensions, such as the region or zone of a workload, the specific pod or node on which a service is running, the customer or organization a request has been issued for, or the topic ID or shard of a message on a queue.

Attributes in OpenTelemetry have some straightforward requirements. A given attribute key can point to a single string, Boolean, floating point, or signed integer value. It can also point to an array of homogeneous values of the same types. This is an important thing to keep in mind, as attribute *keys* cannot be duplicated. If you want to assign multiple values to a single key, you need to use an array.

Attributes are not infinite, and you should be careful when using them on different types of telemetry. By default, any single piece of telemetry can have no more than 128 unique attributes in OpenTelemetry; there's no limit on how long those values can be.

There are two reasons for these requirements. First, it's not free to create or assign an attribute. The OpenTelemetry SDK needs to allocate memory for each attribute, and it can be very easy to accidentally run out of memory in the event of unexpected behavior or code errors. (Incidentally, these are extremely challenging crashes to diagnose, because you're also losing your telemetry about what's happening.) Second, when adding attributes to metric instruments, you can quickly trigger what's known as a *cardinality explosion* when sending them to a time-series database.

Each unique combination of metric name and attribute value creates a new time series, as shown in Figure 3-4. Thus, if you create attributes that each have thousands or millions of values, then the number of created time series can increase exponentially, causing resource starvation or crashes on your metric backend. Regardless of the signal type, attributes are unique to each point or record. Thousands of attributes per span, log, or point would quickly balloon not only memory but also bandwidth, storage, and CPU utilization when telemetry is being created, processed, and exported.

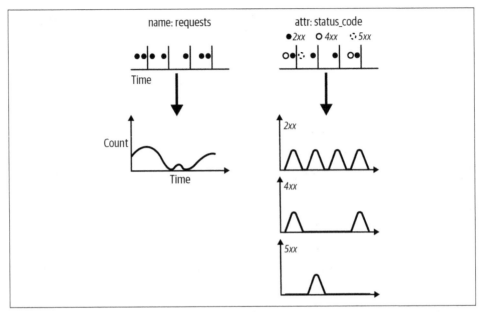

Figure 3-4. Cardinality in action. Adding attributes to a metric creates a unique time series for each combination of attribute values. In this example, the cardinality of status_code *is 3, so it has only three time series. If you added an attribute such as* customer_id *with thousands or millions of variations, this would turn into many thousands or millions of time series!*

There are two ways to manage attribute cardinality. The first is to use observability pipelines, views, and other tools to reduce the cardinality of metrics, traces, and logs as they're emitted and processed. OpenTelemetry is specifically designed for this use case, especially in the case of metrics. We'll have a more detailed explanation of this method in 5 and 6.

Additionally, you can omit attributes from metrics with high cardinality and use those keys on spans or logs instead. Spans and logs generally do not suffer from the cardinality explosions we've mentioned, and in general, more structured metadata about what one of these signals represents is very good to have! You can ask far more interesting questions about your data, and you can build real semantic understanding of what's going on in a system by crafting accurate and descriptive custom attributes for your services.

OpenTelemetry also defines a special type of attribute called a *resource*. The difference between an attribute and a resource is straightforward: attributes can change from one request to the next, but resources remain the same for the entire life of a process. For example, a server's hostname would be a resource attribute, while a customer ID would not be. We'll talk more about creating resource attributes in Chapters 5 and 6.

Semantic Conventions

Several years ago, during a meeting between the maintainers of Prometheus and OpenTelemetry, an unnamed Prometheus maintainer quipped, "You know, I'm not sure about the rest of this, but these semantic conventions are the most valuable thing I've seen in a while." It may sound a bit silly, but it's also true.

System operators are forced to contend with a significant amount of toil simply to ensure that attribute keys, values, and what they represent are the *same* across multiple clouds, application runtimes, hardware architectures, and versions of frameworks and libraries. The OpenTelemetry Semantic Conventions (*https://oreil.ly/semconv*) are designed to remove this consistent point of friction and offer developers a single well-known and well-defined set of attribute keys and values. As of this writing, these conventions are being driven toward stability. Indeed, by the time you read this, we hope that many of them will be stable.

There are two main sources of semantic conventions. The first source is the set of conventions that the project itself describes and ships. These conventions are versioned independently of other OpenTelemetry components, and each version includes a schema that lists validation and transformation rules (see "Compatibility and Future-Proofing" later in this chapter for more information). They are designed to cover most common resources and concepts in cloud native software. For example, the semantic conventions for exceptions define how exceptions and stack traces should be recorded in a span or log. This is useful for developers writing instrumentation code or observability frontends, as they can create user interfaces that support this semantic data.

The other source of conventions is platform teams and other internal sources. Since OpenTelemetry is extensible and composable, you can write a semantic conventions library yourself that includes attributes and values that are specific to your technology stack or services. This is hugely beneficial for organizations with centralized observability teams, since it lets them provide tools to ensure that telemetry data has consistent attributes across teams. This also means that they can leverage the telemetry schema concepts we'll discuss in a few pages to provide migrations as their own internal schemas change. This reduces the burden placed on maintainers of internal platforms—instead of pages of rewrite rules and regular expressions, they can use built-in OpenTelemetry functions to apply transforms.

Third-party library and framework developers also benefit from semantic conventions. Semantic conventions allow them to "ship their observability" alongside their software, giving users well-defined attributes to monitor and alert on. In the future, we hope to see more work along these lines similar to OpenSLO (*https://openslo.com*) and OpenFeature (*https://openfeature.dev*), giving users an open standard for defining alerts, dashboards, and queries across OpenTelemetry data.

OpenTelemetry Protocol

One of the most exciting features of OpenTelemetry is that it provides a standard data format and protocol for observability data. OpenTelemetry Protocol (OTLP) (*https:// oreil.ly/Ad6TE*) offers a single well-supported wire format (how data is stored in memory or sent across the network) for telemetry to be transmitted between agents, services, and backends. It can be sent or received in both binary and text-based encoding and aims to use low amounts of CPU and memory. In practice, OTLP offers significant benefits to an array of telemetry producers and consumers.[5]

Producers of telemetry are able to target OTLP through a thin translation layer between their existing telemetry export formats, making it compatible with a huge array of existing systems. Hundreds of integrations of this sort now exist, such as OTLP through AWS Kinesis Streams (*https://oreil.ly/Bb6CY*), or the contrib receivers (*https://oreil.ly/aMsdQ*) for the OpenTelemetry Collector. In addition, this translation may remap existing attributes into their specified semantic conventions, ensuring data consistency between old and new.

Consumers of telemetry can use OTLP with dozens of open source and commercial tools (*https://oreil.ly/zpH7T*), freeing them from proprietary lock-in. OTLP can be exported to flat files or columnar stores as well, or even to event queues such as Kafka, allowing for nearly endless customization of telemetry data and observability pipelines.

Finally, OTLP is a living part of the OpenTelemetry project. New signals will require updates, but it remains backward compatible with legacy receivers and exporters, ensuring that investments will not go to waste over time. While upgrades to the data format might be required to take advantage of new features or functionality, you can rest easy knowing that telemetry in OTLP will remain compatible with your analysis tools.

Compatibility and Future-Proofing

The foundation of OpenTelemetry is built on two points: standards-based context and conventions, alongside a universal data format. There will be new signals, new features, and a growing ecosystem of tools and clients—so how do you stay up-to-date, and how can you plan for changes?

The project has devised a rigorous guide to versioning and stability (*https://oreil.ly/ ssE1H*), which guides its thinking and roadmap. In short, there will *never* be an OpenTelemetry v2.0. All updates will continue along the v1.0 line, and while there

---

5 For a full discussion of OTLP, as well as a protocol buffer reference, please see the OpenTelemetry protocol page on GitHub (*https://oreil.ly/openteleproto*).

may be deprecations and changes, they'll take place according to a published time-line. Figure 3-5 shows the long-term support guidelines.

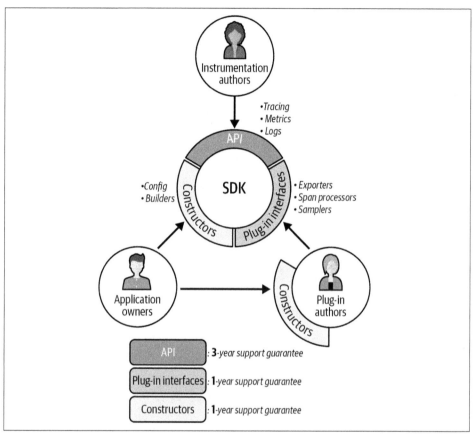

Figure 3-5. OpenTelemetry's long-term support guarantees

OpenTelemetry has a concept of telemetry schemas (*https://oreil.ly/q923o*) to help consumers and producers of telemetry address changes in semantic conventions over time. By building schema-aware analysis tools and storage backends or relying on the OpenTelemetry Collector to perform schema transformations, you can benefit from changes in semantic conventions (and their associated support in analysis tools) without having to reinstrument or redefine output from existing services (see Figure 3-6).

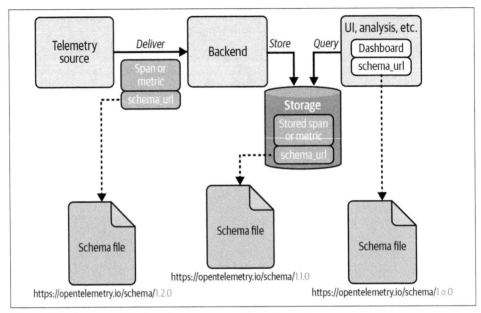

Figure 3-6. An example of a schema-aware telemetry system

Conclusion

Taken in concert, these efforts to provide stability and a seamless upgrade path make OpenTelemetry uniquely suitable to address the challenges faced by large organizations seeking to standardize their telemetry systems and by developers and operators who feel constrained by the limits of existing tooling. Whether you're a single engineer working on a hobby project or a Fortune 10 company building out a multiyear strategy for monitoring and observability, OpenTelemetry can provide a clear and unambiguous answer to the question "What logging/metrics/tracing library should we use?"

CHAPTER 4

The OpenTelemetry Architecture

Everyone knows that debugging is twice as hard as writing a program in the first place. So if you're as clever as you can be when you write it, how will you ever debug it?

—Brian W. Kernighan and P. J. Plauger[1]

OpenTelemetry consists of three kinds of components: instrumentation installed within applications, exporters for infrastructure such as Kubernetes, and pipeline components for sending all of this telemetry to a storage system. You can see how these components connect in Figure 4-1.

This chapter gives you a high-level overview of all the components that make up OpenTelemetry. After that, we'll dive into the OpenTelemetry Demo application to see how the components fit together.

Application Telemetry

The most important source of telemetry is applications. This means that OpenTelemetry must be installed in *every* application for it to work properly. Regardless of whether you install it automatically by using an agent or manually by writing code, the components you'll install are the same. Figure 4-2 shows how they fit together.

---

1 Brian W. Kernighan and P. J. Plauger, *The Elements of Programming Style*, 2nd ed. (New York: McGraw-Hill, 1978).

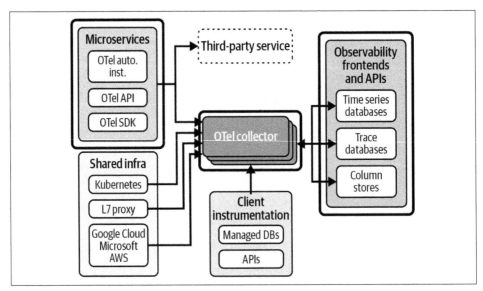

Figure 4-1. The relationship between OpenTelemetry and analysis components

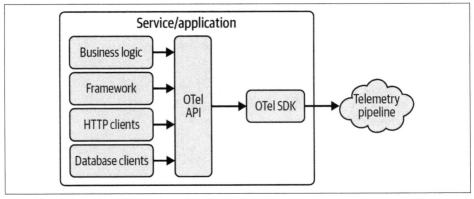

Figure 4-2. OpenTelemetry application architecture

Library Instrumentation

The most critical telemetry comes from OSS libraries such as frameworks, HTTP and RPC clients, and database clients. These libraries perform the heavy lifting in most applications, and often the telemetry from these libraries is sufficient to cover almost all the work that an application performs.

Today, most OSS libraries are not natively instrumented with OpenTelemetry. This means that the instrumentation for these libraries must be installed separately. Open-Telemetry provides instrumentation libraries for many popular OSS libraries.

The OpenTelemetry API

While library instrumentation is very useful, you will inevitably want to instrument critical pieces of application code and business logic. To do this, you use the OpenTelemetry API. The library instrumentation you install is also written with this API, so there is no fundamental difference between application instrumentation and library instrumentation.

In fact, the OpenTelemetry API has a special feature: it is safe to call even when OpenTelemetry is *not* installed within an application. This means that OSS libraries can include OpenTelemetry instrumentation that will automatically be enabled when OpenTelemetry is in use, and that will act as a zero-cost no-op when the library is installed in applications that don't use OpenTelemetry. For more information on how to instrument OSS libraries, see Chapter 6.

The OpenTelemetry SDK

In order for OpenTelemetry API calls sent from libraries and application code to actually be processed, you must install the OpenTelemetry client. We refer to this client as the OpenTelemetry SDK. The SDK is a plug-in framework consisting of sampling algorithms, lifecycle hooks, and exporters that can be configured using environment variables or a YAML configuration file.

Instrumentation Is Critical!

When you think about installing OpenTelemetry in your application, it can be easy to think only about installing only the SDK. It's important to remember that you also need instrumentation for all of your important libraries. As part of installation, be sure to audit your application and confirm that the necessary library instrumentation is available and is installed correctly.

In Chapter 5, we will dive deeper into the innards of these application components and guide you through a successful installation. For now, it's enough to know that these components exist.

Infrastructure Telemetry

Applications run in an environment. In cloud computing, that environment consists of the host the application is running on and the platform used to manage application instances, along with other various networking and database services operated by your cloud provider. Infrastructure health is incredibly important, and large distributed systems have a lot of infrastructure. High-quality telemetry from these services is critical.

OpenTelemetry is slowly being added to Kubernetes and other cloud services. But even without OpenTelemetry, most infrastructure services produce some sort of useful telemetry. OpenTelemetry comes with a number of components that can be used to gather this existing data and add it into the pipeline of telemetry coming from applications. (For more information, see Chapter 7.)

Telemetry Pipelines

The telemetry collected from applications and infrastructure must be sent to an observability tool for storage and analysis. This can turn into a difficult problem in its own right. The amount of telemetry from a large distributed system under heavy load can be enormous. As a result, networking issues such as egress, load balancing, and backpressure can be significant.

In addition, large systems tend to be old systems. This means they may have a patchwork of observability tools in place, have a variety of data-handling requirements, and in general require telemetry to be heavily processed and diverted to various locations. The resulting topology can be very complicated.

To handle this, OpenTelemetry has two primary components: OpenTelemetry Protocol (OTLP), discussed in Chapter 3, and the Collector, which is covered in detail in Chapter 8.

What's Not Included in OpenTelemetry

What OpenTelemetry does *not* include is almost as critical as what it *does* include. Long-term storage, analysis, GUIs, and other frontend components are not included and never will be.

Why? *Standardization.* While it is possible to come up with a stable, universal language for describing computer operations, the analysis part of observability will forever be evolving. OpenTelemetry's goal is to work with all analysis tools and to encourage people to build many more advanced and novel tools in the future. As a result, the OpenTelemetry project will never be extended to include some form of "official" observability backend that would be treated as special or different from all the other observability systems in the world. This separation of concerns—standardized telemetry feeding into an ever-evolving landscape of analysis tools—is fundamental to how the OpenTelemetry project views the world.

Hands-On with the OpenTelemetry Demo

Up to this point, our discussion of OpenTelemetry has been very theoretical. To really understand how things fit together in practice, we need to look at an actual application and some real code.

First, here's a quick recap of what you've learned so far:

- OpenTelemetry provides APIs, SDKs, and an ecosystem of tools to create, collect, transform, and ensure the quality of telemetry data.
- OpenTelemetry ensures that telemetry data is portable and interoperable.
- Unlike the old "three pillars" model, OpenTelemetry braids tracing, metrics, logging, and resources together into a single data model. This creates regularized data that is highly correlated and of uniformly high quality.
- OpenTelemetry Semantic Conventions ensure that telemetry from different libraries is consistent and of uniformly high quality.
- OpenTelemetry is just telemetry. It is designed to send data to a variety of storage and analysis tools and enable newer, more advanced analysis tools to be built.

Clearly, OpenTelemetry is a lot of things and has a lot of moving parts. The goal of this book is not simply to teach you how to create a metric or start a span but to help you understand OpenTelemetry *holistically*. The best way to do that is to see it in action in a real application.

Helpfully, the OpenTelemetry project maintains a robust demo app specifically for this purpose. For the rest of the chapter, we are going to walk through a practical example of the OpenTelemetry architecture as implemented by this demo, Astronomy Shop (*https://oreil.ly/demo*). We'll cover the following:

- Installing and running the demo
- Exploring the application architecture and its design
- Using OpenTelemetry data to answer questions about the demo

You can follow along with just the book, but we highly recommend that you actually spin the demo up yourself. This hands-on approach will clear up a lot of questions.

Running the Demo

For this section, you'll want a recent laptop or desktop computer, ideally with 16GB or more of RAM. You'll also need around 20GB of disk space for all the container images. These instructions assume that you have Docker and Git available and configured.

 Stay Up-to-Date

These instructions were written in late 2023 for OpenTelemetry Demo v1.6.0 (*https://oreil.ly/demo1_6_0*) using a 2022 MacBook Pro with an Apple Silicon M2 Max and 32GB of RAM. Look in the OpenTelemetry Demo Documentation (*https://oreil.ly/demo*) for up-to-date installation instructions for newer versions of the demo or to learn how to install it on Kubernetes.

To install:

1. Navigate to the demo's GitHub repository (*https://oreil.ly/ccrBX*) and clone it to your computer.

2. In a terminal, navigate to the root directory of the repository you just cloned and run `make start`.

If this was successful, after several minutes you should see the following output in your terminal:

```
OpenTelemetry Demo is running.
Go to http://localhost:8080 for the demo UI.
Go to http://localhost:8080/jaeger/ui for the Jaeger UI.
Go to http://localhost:8080/grafana/ for the Grafana UI.
Go to http://localhost:8080/loadgen/ for the Load Generator UI.
Go to http://localhost:8080/feature/ for the Feature Flag UI.
```

In a web browser, navigate to `localhost:8080`, and you should see a web page that looks like Figure 4-3.

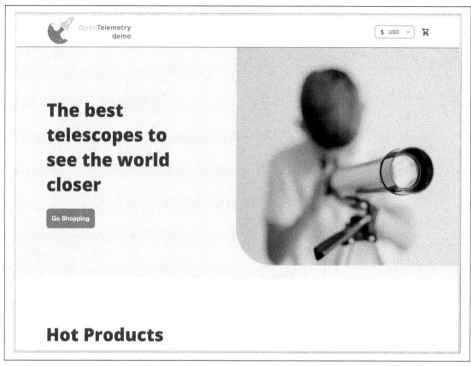

Figure 4-3. The OpenTelemetry Demo front page

If you see this, you're good to go! If you encounter difficulties, check the instructions linked in the note "Stay Up-to-Date" on page 46 for more information and trouble-shooting assistance.

Architecture and Design

Astronomy Shop is a microservice-based ecommerce application composed of 14 separate services, as mapped in Figure 4-4.

The Astronomy Shop is intended to allow developers, operators, and other end users the ability to explore a "production-lite" deployment of a project. To create a useful *demo* with interesting observability examples, some things were included that you wouldn't necessarily see in a "real" production application, such as code designed to simulate failures. Most real-world applications, even the cloud native ones, are significantly more homogeneous than the demo in terms of language and runtime, and a "real" application will usually work with more data layers and storage engines than the demo does.

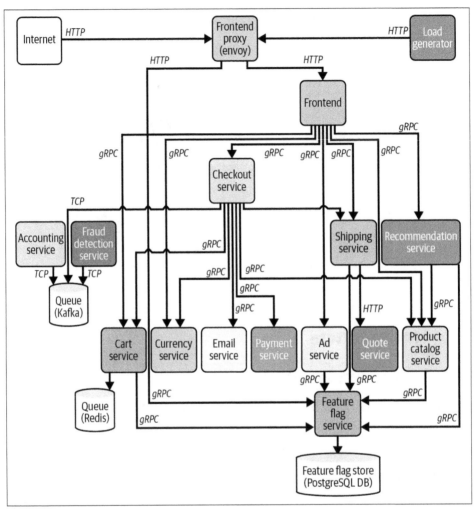

Figure 4-4. The OpenTelemetry Demo service

We can break the overall architecture down into two basic parts: observability concerns and application concerns. The *application concerns* are the services that handle business logic and functional requirements, such as the email service (which handles sending transactional emails to customers) and the currency service (which is responsible for converting between all supported currency values in the application).

Observability concerns are responsible for some part of the overall observability of the application—by collecting and transforming telemetry data, storing and querying it, or visualizing those queries. These concerns include the load generator, the OpenTelemetry Collector, Grafana, Prometheus, Jaeger, and OpenSearch. The load generator is also an observability concern, since it puts a consistent amount of load on the demo application to simulate what a "real-world" environment might look like.

Although the demo is written in a variety of programming languages, its services communicate with each other using a standard framework, in this case gRPC (or JSON Protobuffers over HTTP). This is intentional, for two reasons. First, many organizations (even ones without polyglot environments) standardize around a single RPC framework, such as gRPC. Second, OpenTelemetry supports gRPC and includes useful instrumentation for its libraries out of the box. This means you get a wealth of telemetry data "for free" just by using OpenTelemetry and gRPC.

Managing Application Performance with OpenTelemetry

To see what OpenTelemetry can do, let's create an interesting problem for you to discover. Use your browser to navigate to the Feature Flag UI (`http://local host:8080/feature`) and enable the `cartServiceFailure` and `adServiceFailure` flags by clicking Edit next to each, checking the Enabled checkbox, and then saving your changes. You'll probably want to let the demo run for a few minutes before and after enabling these feature flags, in order to see what performance looks like before and after enabling them. Figure 4-5 shows what you should see in the Feature Flag UI after accomplishing this task.

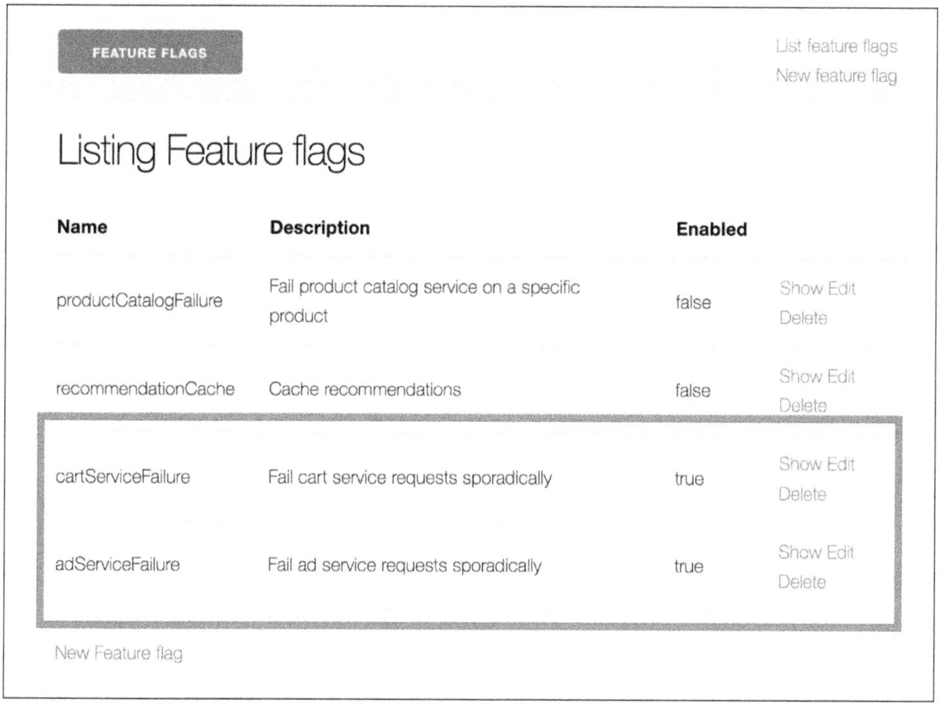

FEATURE FLAGS			List feature flags New feature flag

Listing Feature flags

Name	Description	Enabled	
productCatalogFailure	Fail product catalog service on a specific product	false	Show Edit Delete
recommendationCache	Cache recommendations	false	Show Edit Delete
cartServiceFailure	Fail cart service requests sporadically	true	Show Edit Delete
adServiceFailure	Fail ad service requests sporadically	true	Show Edit Delete

New Feature flag

Figure 4-5. The selected feature flags being enabled in the Feature Flag UI

After waiting a few minutes, you can start exploring the data. Grafana (`http://local host:8080/grafana/`) has several prebuilt dashboards available; one of the more interesting ones is the Spanmetrics Demo Dashboard. This dashboard gives you an "APM-style" view of the services, showing the latency, error rate, and throughput of each route across all application services. What's interesting is that this dashboard is generated not from metrics but from *trace data*, using the OpenTelemetry Collector's `spanmetrics` connector. If you filter this dashboard to the Ad Service and Cart Service (Figure 4-6), you'll notice that they have a slightly elevated error rate—but you'll also see where exactly that error rate lies.

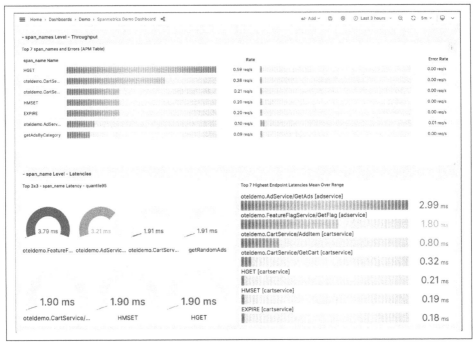

Figure 4-6. The Spanmetrics Dashboard in Grafana

You can see in the chart at bottom right in Figure 4-6 that the name of the span showing the higher error rate is `oteldemo.AdService/GetAds`. That's a useful starting point for an investigation.

How would you normally figure out what's causing this issue? Many people would reach for logs. But because OpenTelemetry is providing rich, high-context traces, you can take the two pieces of data you do have—the presence and the location of errors—and use those to search for traces that match.

In Grafana, you can explore trace data by going to the Explore item in the menu. Once there, select Jaeger from the drop-down menu near the top (it should say Prometheus by default), and then change to a Search query. Input the information that you know, as seen in Figure 4-7, and then click Run Query. You'll see all the requests that include errors for that specific route. Inspecting these traces reveals that a small percentage of transactions are failing with a gRPC error. You could take that information and do further investigation, comparing it with memory or CPU utilization on the host or container.

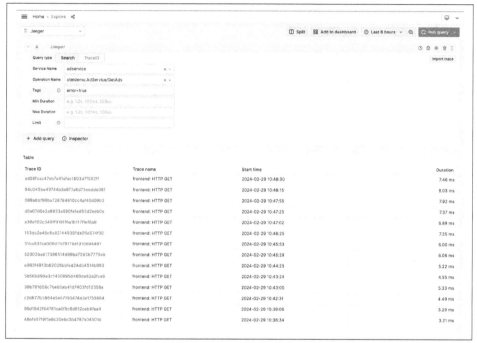

Figure 4-7. Exploring Jaeger trace data in Grafana

While this random error might not be terribly interesting, what *is* interesting is that the instrumentation required to get this result was free, so to speak. This is an example of *automatic instrumentation* (or *zero-code instrumentation*), in which an agent or a library adds instrumentation code without you having to write anything to enable it. If you look at the Dockerfile for the Ad Service, you can see that it downloads an agent as part of the build, copies it into the container, and runs it alongside the service. This means that on startup, the necessary instrumentation is added in without any work on the developer's part.

A similar pattern exists in the Cart Service, and again, you don't have to write the instrumentation required to discover it. In .NET, OpenTelemetry is integrated into the runtime itself—all you have to do is enable it. Look for yourself: open /src/cartservice/src/Program.cs in an editor and look at line 52. We've added some notes to the following code to help you understand what's going on:

```
builder.Services.AddOpenTelemetry() ❶
    .ConfigureResource(appResourceBuilder)
    .WithTracing(tracerBuilder => tracerBuilder
        .AddRedisInstrumentation(
            options => options.SetVerboseDatabaseStatements = true)
        .AddAspNetCoreInstrumentation()
        .AddGrpcClientInstrumentation() ❷
        .AddHttpClientInstrumentation()
        .AddOtlpExporter()) ❸
    .WithMetrics(meterBuilder => meterBuilder ❹
        .AddProcessInstrumentation()
        .AddRuntimeInstrumentation()
        .AddAspNetCoreInstrumentation()
```

❶ This adds OpenTelemetry libraries to the dependency injection container present in .NET applications.

❷ This enables built-in instrumentation for gRPC clients.

❸ Here, we enable OTLP export to send the data to an OpenTelemetry Collector.

❹ We're also getting metrics out—process metrics such as memory and garbage collection, HTTP server metrics, etc.

In both cases, OpenTelemetry provides valuable telemetry at the framework level with very little effort on your part. In Chapter 5 we'll go into more detail on the availability of this kind of automatic instrumentation in other languages—it's not just for .NET and Java!

Finding Needles in Haystacks

Framework instrumentation gets you a lot, as we demonstrated in the last section. You can get a lot more, though, by adding in more instrumentation. Chapters 5 and 6 cover this in more detail, but let's give you a taste of the difference. Figure 4-8 shows the difference between framework instrumentation alone and a combination of framework and custom instrumentation in a transaction between two services in the demo.

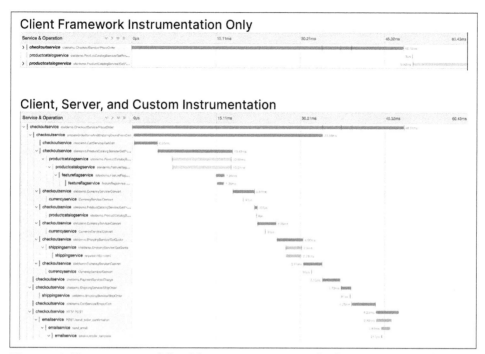

Figure 4-8. Two trace waterfalls of the same transaction. The first trace (at top) demonstrates client spans only; the second includes client, server, and custom spans.

Let's investigate a problem that can be found only with custom instrumentation. If you go back to the Feature Flag UI (`http://localhost:8080/feature`) and enable `productCatalogFailure`, you'll introduce a new issue to the demo. After a few minutes, you'll notice that the error rate for several services is starting to creep up, especially for the frontend (Figure 4-9).

This is emblematic of a pretty common failure mode in distributed applications: *the thing that's failing isn't necessarily the thing that has a problem*. If this was a real application, your frontend team would probably be getting paged for that relatively high error rate. Your first port of call might be a basic health check for the frontend, which is available in the demo as the `httpcheck.status` metric. Querying that in Grafana, though, shows that everything is fine (Figure 4-10).

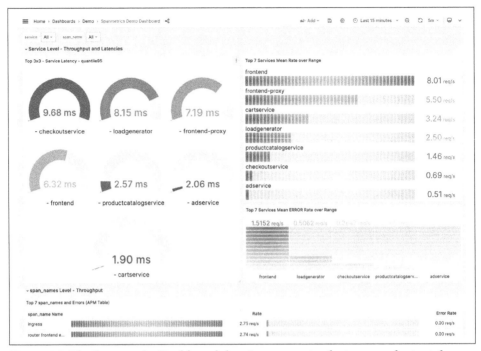

Figure 4-9. The Spanmetrics Dashboard showing error rates during a product catalog service failure

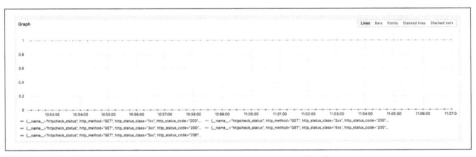

Figure 4-10. Querying the `httpcheck.status` *metric in Grafana*

This tells you that the web server isn't having problems. Perhaps it's the frontend service? If you had only metrics and logs to work with, you would need to start searching through log statements, trying to pick out the errors. Since span metrics are available, though, you can instead look for errors by *route* (Figure 4-11). By filtering for just frontend spans and restricting it to just errors, you can add up those errors across all the calls the frontend is making into the backend.

Here's something interesting: the spike in errors is coming from the product catalog service! If you're a frontend dev, you can breathe easy; it's probably not your fault.

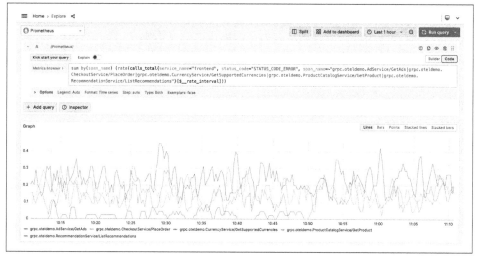

Figure 4-11. Filtering span metrics to find errors by route

Your next step in troubleshooting should be to investigate these specific errors. As before, you can search for spans matching the failure in Grafana or in Jaeger directly.

If you explore all of the traces that call `oteldemo.ProductCatalogService/GetProduct`, you may notice that the errors all have something in common: they happen only when the `app.product.id` attribute is a specific value. In Jaeger and Grafana alone, this fact can be somewhat challenging to discover; you have to compare many traces with each other, either manually or by using single trace comparisons. More advanced analysis tools—both open source and commercial—support aggregate analysis of spans and correlation detection. Using those, you could more easily see the specific value that leads to the error, reducing the time required to identify and remediate the problem.

Now, automatic instrumentation can't know about the domain- or business-specific logic and metadata that matter to your service. You have to add that in yourself by extending the instrumentation. In this case, the product catalog uses gRPC instrumentation. You'll want to attach useful soft context to the spans that it generates, like the particular product ID being requested. You can see where this attribute is set in lines 198 to 202 of the source code (*/src/productcatalogservice/main.go*):

```
func (p *productCatalog) GetProduct(ctx context.Context, req *pb.GetProductRequest)
        (*pb.Product, error) { ❺
    span := trace.SpanFromContext(ctx) ❻
    span.SetAttributes(
            attribute.String("app.product.id", req.Id), ❼
    )
```

❺ In Go, OpenTelemetry context is carried in the Context.

❻ To modify an existing span or start a new one, you need to get the current span from the Context.

❼ Because OpenTelemetry is semantic, you need to strongly type attributes and their values.

There's more to the demo than what we've covered here, including database requests, asynchronous work through Kafka, and infrastructure monitoring. You'd be well served to read through the services in the languages you're most familiar with to get an idea of how you can use OpenTelemetry in practice and explore the data it emits. At the time of this writing, support for all OpenTelemetry features in the demo is somewhat spotty. Tracing works well everywhere, and metrics work in about half of the services. Logging support is offered in a handful of services right now, but by the time you read this, it should be more widespread.

Observability Pipelines in the Demo

The last thing to note about the demo is how it collects data. When possible, the demo prefers to push data from a process to an instance of the OpenTelemetry Collector. Filtering, batching, and creating metric views are all accomplished at the Collector rather than in the process itself.

This is done for two reasons. First, it's a good idea to get telemetry out of your service as quickly as possible. Creating telemetry isn't free; there's some overhead. The more processing you do at the application level, the more overhead you create. This might be fine when things are running well, but unexpected load patterns (like the kind that happen during an incident) can have unexpected outcomes on a service's performance profile. If your application crashes before you can export (or scrape) data, you lose those insights. That said, it's also possible to create so *much* telemetry that it can overwhelm local network links and cause performance issues at a *different* layer of your system. There's no absolute rule here—everyone will have different circumstances. Your best bet is to ensure that you enable good metamonitoring of your OpenTelemetry infrastructure. (You can see an example of this in the Collector dashboard included in the demo.) There's a much more comprehensive discussion of observability pipelines in Chapter 8.

The New Observability Model

Now that you've seen an application that uses OpenTelemetry, let's review how everything we've talked about so far fits together. The rest of this book will focus on more of the specifics. You can think of this section as the "end of the beginning."

We talked in Chapter 1 about the "three browser tabs of observability," but the concept is worth revisiting in more detail. People use observability tools out of necessity more than anything else. While it's nice to wax philosophic about data modeling strategies or mapping systems to telemetry signals, they usually don't have a big impact on your actual day-to-day work. If you think about them that way, then it makes sense as to why most tools are vertically integrated. They're integrated because doing so is the most cost-efficient set of trade-offs for the people who build them.

Let's take a specific example around metrics. If you're building a metrics analysis and storage tool, then you'll probably want to create some efficiencies in your system, especially for things that appear frequently. You can do this with strategies for clustering, reaggregation, and compaction. Accomplishing this, though, requires that you control the instrumentation and collection pipeline—you need to make sure you're adding the right attributes to the right data. Other efficiencies come out of this: for instance, you could reduce the process overhead for generating metrics by moving attribute generation to an external process, stateless wire formats, and so forth.

A lot of that goes out the window once you're dealing with a data pipeline you no longer control, though. This is why OpenTelemetry is such a big deal in the observability space: it breaks this fundamental model. The result is a new model of observability tooling that opens the door to significant innovation.

In the model pictured in Figure 4-12, the "new" way of doing things is built on a foundation of unified, universal instrumentation via OpenTelemetry. It combines telemetry from all your sources—greenfield code, legacy code, existing instrumentation, and business data from systems of record and other important sources. This data is then sent to (at least) one data store via OTLP.

OpenTelemetry acts as a universal conduit for telemetry data, allowing you to process and send telemetry streams based on any number of factors, such as the value of the data to your business or the use case you'd like to enable with it. It's a critical building block for what can come next.

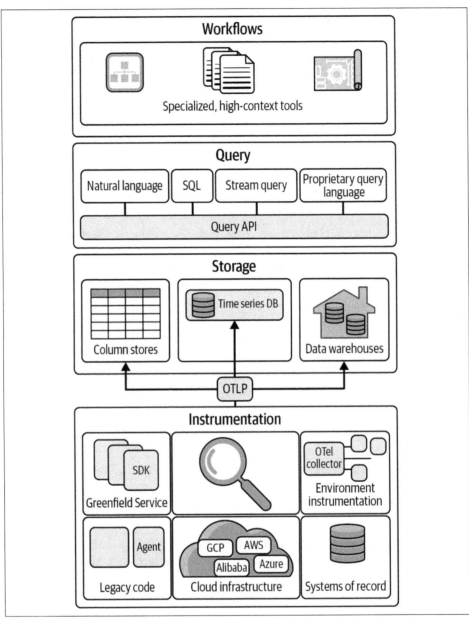

Figure 4-12. The new model of observability tools

Future observability platforms will offer capabilities such as universal query APIs, letting you seamlessly fetch telemetry data from a variety of data stores. Rather than being locked into a single query language, you'll be able to use natural language—with assistance from AI tools—to easily find what you're looking for. Rather than being restricted to large omnibus platforms, you'll be able to select from a wide range of specific analysis tools designed to solve particular problems, thanks to the data portability OpenTelemetry offers.

OpenTelemetry isn't going to solve these problems by itself, but it's a critical part of the solution. In some ways, it's designed more for this future of highly contextual data and tools capable of understanding it than the tools of today are.

You may have felt the dissonance between the "old" and "new" ways of doing things in the previous section. For as much as we've talked (and will continue to talk) about metrics and logs, a lot of the demo workflows are built around tracing. Some of this is because the tools that we have, such as Prometheus and Jaeger, just don't support the sort of high-cardinality, highly contextual workflows that OpenTelemetry provides. All OpenTelemetry components are designed to work together and can be extended to level up your existing telemetry data without reinstrumentation. However, to really get the most value from this, your tools also need to support the concepts of high-cardinality data, correlation across hard and soft contexts, and unified telemetry.

As of this writing, there are excellent signs of progress in that direction. A raft of new observability tools have launched over the past couple of years, many of which rely exclusively on OpenTelemetry for instrumentation. These tools, built on open source column stores, are all well suited to the kind of highly contextual telemetry data that OpenTelemetry provides. Large organizations are adopting OpenTelemetry as well, including Microsoft and Amazon Web Services, both of which recently announced first-class support for OpenTelemetry (for Microsoft as part of Azure Monitor, and for Amazon as an OpenTelemetry-powered APM experience for EKS applications). Noncommercial tools are ramping up their OpenTelemetry support as well, with projects like OpenSearch and ClickHouse becoming more and more popular for storing OpenTelemetry data.

Conclusion

Understanding the basic building blocks of OpenTelemetry and seeing how they fit together in a real application is your first real step into practical OpenTelemetry. Now that you've gotten your feet wet, it's time to dive into the details.

The rest of the book is dedicated to the specifics of how OpenTelemetry works and what you need to know to successfully instrument your applications, libraries, and infrastructure for observability. We'll also cover practical advice on how to design telemetry pipelines and roll out observability to an organization, based on case studies from existing users. After each deep dive, we'll include a checklist you can follow to help make sure your OpenTelemetry rollout is successful.

CHAPTER 5

Instrumenting Applications

It is easier to write an incorrect program than understand a correct one.
—Alan J. Perlis[1]

Adding OpenTelemetry to all of your application services is an important part of getting started—and it's definitely the most complex part. The process of setting up OpenTelemetry is twofold: installing the software development kit (SDK) and installing instrumentation. The SDK is the OpenTelemetry client responsible for processing and exporting the telemetry. *Instrumentation* is code written using the OpenTelemetry API to generate telemetry.

Instrumenting applications can be difficult and time-consuming. While some languages can automate this process, it's very helpful to understand what the components actually are and how they relate to each other. Occasionally there are problems with installation, and it's very difficult to debug a system you aren't familiar with!

This book does not provide detailed setup instructions or code snippets. That's what the documentation (*https://oreil.ly/docs*) is for, and we don't want to provide instructions that could be out-of-date by the time you read this. Instead, in this chapter we'll provide a high-level overview of the entire installation process, descriptions of the components involved, and advice on what we consider to be best practices. Read this before you begin so you will better understand the goals you are trying to reach and know what to look for in the documentation.

It's also possible to overinstrument an application, or to spend too much time instrumenting one service before moving on to the next one. Check out the advice in "How Much Is Too Much?" on page 75 to understand when to stop.

---

1 Alan J. Perlis, "Epigrams on Programming," *SIGPLAN Notices* 17, no. 9 (September 1982): 7–13.

Near the end of this chapter, you will find a complete setup checklist. Reviewing a checklist before deploying OpenTelemetry is an extremely helpful way to ensure that everything is working properly. Even if you already know how to install OpenTelemetry, we recommend that you share this checklist with your team and use it every time you instrument an application.

Agents and Automated Setup

In all languages, you need to install two parts: the SDK that processes and exports telemetry, and all the instrumentation libraries that match the frameworks, database clients, and other common components used by your application. That's a lot of pieces to install and set up. Ideally, we would want to automate all of this work.

But when it comes to *automation*, every language is different. Some languages provide complete automation that requires no code at all. Other languages provide no automation whatsoever. While we don't want to go into details (again, read the docs!), we do believe that before you get started, it's helpful to understand what kind of automation is available.

The following languages provide additional tooling for auto-instrumentation. When you install OpenTelemetry for the first time, we recommend you read the docs on these tools and learn how to use them:

Java
> The OpenTelemetry Java agent (*https://oreil.ly/KyB6Y*) can automatically install the SDK and all available instrumentation via the standard `-javaagent` command-line argument.

.NET
> The .NET instrumentation agent (*https://oreil.ly/2QvzL*) automatically installs the SDK and available instrumentation packages and is run alongside a .NET application itself.

Node.js
> The @opentelemetry/auto-instrumentations-node package (*https://oreil.ly/wZff2*) can automatically install the SDK and all available instrumentation via the `node --require` flag.

PHP
> For PHP 8.0 and greater, OpenTelemetry can automatically install the SDK and all available instrumentation via the OpenTelemetry PHP extension (*https://oreil.ly/icFTC*).

Python

The opentelemetry-instrumentation package (*https://oreil.ly/MncRd*) can auto-matically install the SDK and all available instrumentation via the `opentelemetry-instrument` command.

Ruby

The opentelemetry-instrumentation-all package (*https://oreil.ly/XedtM*) can auto-matically install all available instrumentation, but you'll still need to set up and configure the OpenTelemetry SDK.

Go

The OpenTelemetry Go Instrumentation package (*https://oreil.ly/wlW_0*) uses eBPF to instrument popular Go libraries. Future work should allow it to extend manual instrumentation and set up an SDK for you.

Installing the SDK

In some languages—for example, Rust and Erlang—automation does not exist. You install and set up the OpenTelemetry SDK just like any other library. Even in languages in which auto-instrumentation is available, you may want to set things up by hand in order to have more control. Auto-instrumentation can sometimes come with extra overhead, and you may eventually want to customize the installation beyond what the automation will let you do.

So how do you install the SDK? You construct and configure a set of providers and register them with the OpenTelemetry API. This process is described next.

Registering Providers

What happens if you make an OpenTelemetry API call? By default, nothing. That API call is a *no-op*, meaning that the API is safe to call, but nothing happens and there is no overhead.

For something to happen, you need to register providers with the API. A *provider* is an implementation of the OpenTelemetry instrumentation API. These providers handle all of the API calls. The TracerProvider creates tracers and spans. The MeterProvider creates meters and instruments. The LoggerProvider creates loggers. As OpenTelemetry expands in scope, more providers may be added in the future.

You should register providers as early as possible in the application boot cycle. Any API calls made before registering a provider will be no-ops and will not be recorded.

Why Have Providers?

This provider business seems extra complicated. Why is OpenTelemetry separated like this? There are two main reasons.

One reason is that separate providers allow you to be selective and install only the parts of OpenTelemetry that you plan on using. For example, let's say you already have a metrics and logs solution for your application, and you want to use OpenTelemetry only to add tracing. This is easy to do without ending up with an extra metrics and logging system: just install the OpenTelemetry tracing provider by itself. The metric and logging instrumentation will remain no-ops.

The second main reason is loose coupling. Registering providers allows the API to be completely separate from the implementation. The API packages contain only interfaces and constants. They have almost no dependencies and are very lightweight. This means that libraries that use the OpenTelemetry API do not automatically pull in a huge dependency chain. This is helpful for avoiding dependency conflicts in shared libraries that run in many applications.

An additional reason is flexibility. If you want to use OpenTelemetry instrumentation but don't like our implementation, you don't have to use it. You can write your own implementation and register that with the API instead of using the SDK. (See "Custom Providers" on page 70 this chapter).

Providers

When we talk about the SDK, we're talking about a set of provider implementations. Each provider is a framework that can be extended and configured through various types of plug-ins, as described in the following sections.

TracerProvider

A *TracerProvider* implements the OpenTelemetry tracing API. It consists of samplers, SpanProcessors, and exporters. Figure 5-1 shows how these components relate to one another.

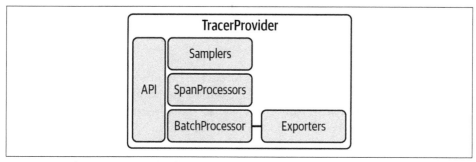

```
                    TracerProvider
         ┌─────────────────────────────────┐
         │         │  ┌──────────────────┐  │
         │         │  │    Samplers      │  │
         │         │  └──────────────────┘  │
         │   API   │  ┌──────────────────┐  │
         │         │  │  SpanProcessors  │  │
         │         │  └──────────────────┘  │
         │         │  ┌──────────────┐ ┌──────────┐
         │         │  │BatchProcessor│─│ Exporters│
         │         │  └──────────────┘ └──────────┘
         └─────────────────────────────────┘
```

Figure 5-1. The TracerProvider framework

Samplers

Samplers choose whether the span is recorded or dropped. A variety of sampling algorithms are available, and choosing which sampler to use and how to configure it is one of the most confusing parts of setting up a tracing system.

Dropped or Recorded?

Calling a span "sampled" can mean it was "sampled out" (dropped) or "sampled in" (recorded), so it's good to be specific.

It's difficult to choose a sampler without understanding how you plan to use the telemetry. Sampling means losing data. What data is safe to lose? If you're trying to measure only average latency, a random sampler that records only one out of 1,024 traces will work fine and could save quite a bit of money. But if you want to investigate edge cases and outliers—extreme latency, rare but dangerous errors—a random sampler will lose too much data and could miss recording these events.

This means that the sampler you choose will very much depend on the kind of features available in the tracing analysis tool to which you are sending the telemetry. If you sample in a manner that is incompatible with your analysis tool, you'll get misleading data and nonfunctional features. We strongly recommend that you consult with the vendor of the tracing or OSS product you're using for advice on sampling.

When in doubt, do not sample at all. It's better to start out without any sampling and then add it later in response to specific costs or overhead you are looking to reduce. Don't reflexively add a sampler until you understand the costs you are trying to reduce and the kinds of sampling your tracing product is compatible with. (For a more complete discussion of sampling, check out "Filtering and Sampling" on page 116.)

SpanProcessors

SpanProcessors allow you to collect and modify spans. They intercept the span twice: once when it starts and once when it ends.

The default processor is called a *BatchProcessor*. This processor buffers span data and manages the exporter plug-ins described in the following subsection. Generally, you should install the BatchProcessor as the last SpanProcessor in your processing pipeline. BatchProcessors have the following configuration options:

exporter
> The exporter to which the spans are pushed.

maxQueueSize
> The maximum number of spans held in the buffer. Any further spans are dropped. The default value is 2,048.

scheduledDelayMillis
> The delay interval in milliseconds between two consecutive exports. The default value is 5,000.

exportTimeoutMillis
> How long an export can run before it is canceled. The default value is 30,000.

maxExportBatchSize
> The maximum number of spans in an export. If the queue reaches maxExport BatchSize, a batch will be exported even if scheduledDelayMillis has not elapsed. The default value is 512.

Most default values are fine. But if telemetry is being exported to a local Collector, we recommend setting scheduledDelayMillis to a much smaller number. This ensures that you'll lose only a minimal amount of telemetry data if the application suddenly crashes. The default value (five seconds) can also slow things down and create confusion during development, because you have to sit there and wait five seconds every time you want to test a change you made.

As time goes on, you may find it useful to write additional SpanProcessors to modify span attributes or integrate spans with other systems. However, most processing that can be done in a SpanProcessor can also be done later, in a Collector. This is preferable; it's best to do as little processing in the application as possible. Then you can use a local Collector for any further buffering, processing, and exporting. It's also helpful to run a local Collector to capture machine metrics and additional resources (see Chapter 8), so this is a very common setup.

Exporters

How do you get all these spans out of a process and into something you can read? Exporters! These plug-ins define the format and destination of your telemetry data.

The default is to use the OpenTelemetry Protocol (OTLP) exporter, which we recommend. The only situation in which you should *not* use OTLP is when you are not running a Collector and are sending data directly to an analysis tool that does not support OTLP. In that case, check the analysis tool documentation to find out which exporter is compatible.

Here are the OTLP configuration options that you should be aware of:

protocol
OTLP supports three transport protocols: gRPC, `http/protobuf`, and `http/json`. We recommend `http/protobuf`, which is also the default.

endpoint
The URL to which the exporter is going to send spans or metrics. The default values are `http://localhost:4318` for HTTP and `http://localhost:4317` for gRPC.

headers
Additional HTTP headers added to every export request. Some analysis tools may require an account or security token header to route data correctly.

compression
Used to turn on GZip compression. This is recommended for larger batch sizes.

timeout
> The maximum time the OTLP exporter will wait for each batch export. It defaults to 10 seconds.

certificate file, client key file, and client certificate file
> Used for verifying a server's TLS credentials when a secure connection is required.

MeterProvider

A *MeterProvider* implements the OpenTelemetry metrics API. It consists of views, MetricReaders, MetricProducers, and MetricExporters. Figure 5-2 shows how these components relate to one another.

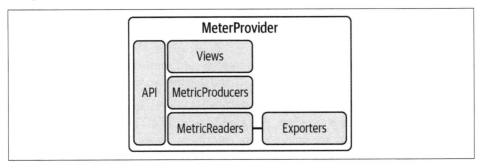

Figure 5-2. The MeterProvider framework

MetricReaders

MetricReaders are the metric equivalent of SpanProcessors. They collect and buffer metric data until it can be exported. The default MetricReader is a `PeriodicExpor` `tingMetricReader`. This reader collects metric data and then pushes it to an exporter in batches. Use it when exporting OTLP. Periodic readers have two configuration options you should be aware of:

`exportIntervalMillis`
> The time interval in milliseconds between two consecutive exports. The default value is 60,000.

`exportTimeoutMillis`
> How long the export can run before it is canceled. The default value is 30,000.

MetricProducers

It is common for existing applications to already have metric instrumentation of some kind. You need *MetricProducers* to connect some types of third-party instrumentation to an OpenTelemetry SDK, so that you can start mixing your existing instrumentation with new OpenTelemetry instrumentation. For example, Prometheus instrumentation may require a MetricProducer.

Every MetricProducer is registered with a MetricReader. If you have existing metric instrumentation, check the documentation to learn which MetricProducer is required to connect it to the OpenTelemetry SDK.

MetricExporters

MetricExporters send batches of metrics over the network. As with traces, we recommend using the OTLP exporter to send telemetry to a Collector.

If you are a Prometheus user and are not using a Collector, then you'll want to use Prometheus's pull-based collection system instead of the push-based system used by OTLP. Installing the Prometheus exporter will set this up.

If you are first sending data to a Collector, then use the OTLP exporter in your application and install the Prometheus exporter in the Collector. We recommend this approach.

Views

Views are a powerful tool for customizing the metrics the SDK outputs. You can choose which instruments are ignored, how an instrument aggregates data, and which attributes are reported.

When you are just getting started, there is no need to configure views; you may never need to touch them. Later, when you are fine-tuning metrics and looking to lower your overhead, you might want to look into creating your first views. You also don't necessarily have to create views at the SDK level—you can use the OpenTelemetry Collector to create them as well.

LoggerProvider

A *LoggerProvider* implements the OpenTelemetry logging API. It consists of LogRecordProcessors and LogRecordExporters. Figure 5-3 shows how these components relate to one another.

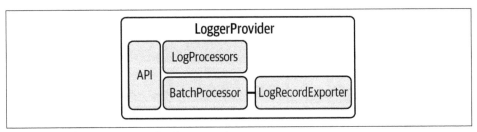

Figure 5-3. The LoggerProvider framework

LogRecordProcessors

LogRecordProcessors work just like SpanProcessors. The default processor is a batch processor, which you use to register your exporters. As with the span batch processor, we recommend lowering the `scheduledDelayMillis` config parameter when sending data to a local Collector.

LogRecordExporters

LogRecordExporters emit logging data in a variety of common formats. As with the other signals, we recommend using the OTLP exporter.

Shutting Down Providers

When shutting down an application, it's critical to flush any remaining telemetry before the application terminates. *Flushing* is the process of immediately exporting any remaining telemetry data already buffered in the SDK while blocking shutdown. If your application terminates before flushing the SDK, you could lose critical observability data.

To perform a final flush, every SDK provider includes a Shutdown method. Make sure to integrate this method into your application shutdown procedure as one of the final steps.

Automatic Shutdown

If you're using automatic instrumentation through an agent, the agent will call shutdown as a process exits, so you don't need to do anything.

Custom Providers

The SDK we've described is what the OpenTelemetry project recommends using with the OpenTelemetry API. These frameworks provide a balance of flexibility and efficiency, and in most scenarios they work just fine.

However, for some edge cases, the SDK architecture may not be appropriate. In these rare cases, it's possible to create your own alternative implementation. Allowing alternative implementations is one of the reasons the OpenTelemetry API is separate from the SDK.

For example, the OpenTelemetry C++ SDK is multithreaded. Envoy, a popular proxy service, makes use of the OpenTelemetry API for instrumentation. However, Envoy requires that all its components be single-threaded. It's not feasible to make the SDK optionally single-threaded; that would mean an entirely different architecture. So, in this case, a separate single-threaded implementation was written in C++ to work with Envoy.

It's highly unlikely that you'll need to build a custom implementation. We list the option for completeness and to help clarify why OpenTelemetry keeps a strict separation of concerns between the instrumentation interfaces and their implementation.

Configuration Best Practices

You can configure the SDK in three ways:

- In code, when constructing exporters, samplers, and processors
- Using environment variables
- Using a YAML config file

The most widely supported method of configuring the OpenTelemetry SDK or automatic instrumentation is through environment variables. This is better than hard coding configuration options within an application, because it allows operators to set these values at deployment time. This is a critical feature, since the correct OpenTelemetry configuration options can vary greatly among development, testing, and production environments. For example, in development, you might send data to a local Collector to verify your installation. In testing, you might send data directly to a small-scale analysis tool designed to test-load and alert for performance regressions. Then, in production, you might send data to a load balancer specific to the network to which that particular application instance has been deployed.

Also, in production, telemetry pipelines can generate a lot of data, so they require a setup that can handle high throughput. You may need to tune several parameters to avoid overwhelming your telemetry pipeline. Sending more data than the system can actually process is called *backpressure*, and it will lead to dropped telemetry.

Recently, the OpenTelemetry project defined a config file that works across all languages. This is the new recommended approach for configuration. A config file has all the advantages of environment variables but is much easier to check and verify. It is also easy to create config file templates for developers and operators to follow.

The same config file format works across all OpenTelemetry implementations. If necessary, you can still use environment variables to override any settings listed in the config file. As of this writing, support for this new configuration file is mixed, but we expect it to increase.

Remote Configuration

As we write this, OpenTelemetry is developing Open Agent Management Protocol (OpAMP), a remote configuration protocol for Collectors and SDKs. OpAmp will allow Collectors and SDKs to open a port, through which they transmit their current status and receive configuration updates. Using OpAMP, a control plane can manage the entire OpenTelemetry deployment without the need to restart or redeploy.

Some configuration options, such as sampling, are highly dependent on what telemetry data is being generated and how it is being used. With OpAMP, an analysis tool could control these settings dynamically, dropping any data that is not being used early in the telemetry pipeline. This can mean enormous cost savings in large deployments, because you can tune the data collected precisely to match the data required to run the features the analysis tool provides. As we mention later, configuring sampling by hand is difficult and not recommended unless you understand the type of sampling your analysis tool is compatible with.

Attaching Resources

Resources are a set of attributes that define the environment in which telemetry is being collected. They describe the service, the virtual machine, the platform, the region, the cloud provider—everything you need to know to correlate production problems with a particular location or service. If your telemetry data, such as spans, metrics, and logs, tells you *what* is happening, resources tell you *where* it is happening.

Resource Detectors

Beyond the service-specific resources, most resources come from the environment in which the application is deployed, such as Kubernetes, AWS, GCP, Azure, or Linux. These resources come from a known location and usually have a standard way of being acquired. Plug-ins that discover these resources are called *resource detectors.*

When setting up OpenTelemetry, make a list of every aspect of your environment you want to capture, and then investigate whether a resource detector already exists to capture this information. Most resources can be discovered by a local Collector and attached to the telemetry coming from an application as it passes through the Collector.

Almost all OpenTelemetry SDKs, regardless of language, include resource detectors. Accessing some resources requires API calls, which can slow application startup, so we recommend the Collector approach.

Service Resources

There's one critical set of resources you can't gather from the environment: the resources that describe your service. These resources are incredibly important, so make sure you define them as part of setting up OpenTelemetry. They include the following:

service.name
> The name of this class of service—for example, frontend or payment-processor.

service.namespace
> Service names are not always globally unique. A service namespace can help differentiate two different types of "frontend" service.

service.instance.id
> The unique ID that describes this particular instance, written in whatever format you use for generating unique IDs.

service.version
> The version number, written in whatever format you use for versioning.

Again, it is *vitally important* to set these resources. Many analysis tools require them in order to provide certain features. For example, let's say you want to compare performance of different versions of an application and identify any regressions. If you haven't recorded the service.version, there will be no way to do this.

Advanced Resource Annotation Strategies

Depending on the eventual destination of your telemetry streams, consider carefully how you place resource detection in your Collector pipelines. For example, perhaps you want to keep high-fidelity data from a Kubernetes cluster available in that cluster for a short time, while shipping the rest of it to a persistent store. In this case, you might apply resource detection and annotation only to the latter telemetry streams. It wouldn't be important for the other streams, since the high-fidelity telemetry would be local to the cluster on which it was viewed. Please see Chapter 8 for more details on setting up telemetry pipelines.

Installing Instrumentation

Besides the SDK, OpenTelemetry requires instrumentation. Ideally, you should not have to write any of this instrumentation yourself. If your application is built out of common libraries (HTTP clients, web frameworks, messaging clients, database clients), their instrumentation should be sufficient to get you started.

Auto-instrumentation can help you find and install instrumentation for these libraries. If none is available, make a list of all the major libraries your application uses and compare it with the list of available instrumentation. You can find instrumentation information in the Registry section of the OpenTelemetry website (*https:// oreil.ly/lGG48*) and in the "contrib" repository for each language in the OpenTelemetry GitHub organization (*https://github.com/open-telemetry*).

Each instrumentation package includes installation instructions for how to install it. Failing to install a critical instrumentation package is the most common way to break traces.

Native Instrumentation

More and more OSS libraries are starting to include OpenTelemetry instrumentation within the library itself. This means that no additional instrumentation needs to be installed. As soon as you install the SDK, OpenTelemetry will work out of the box for this library! For more details, see Chapter 6.

Instrumenting Application Code

You may want to instrument your in-house libraries as well as the application code itself.

To instrument in-house libraries, see Chapter 6 and follow the same pattern. This is the best approach to instrumentation. Ideally, instrumentation can remain in these shared libraries, and you won't have to add instrumentation directly to application code, outside of adding attributes that help describe the business logic they're implementing. You don't want to spend your time rewriting the same instrumentation in every application!

Decorating Spans

Developers may want to add application-specific details to help track down issues and index their spans. As a reminder, there is no need to add an additional span when you want to do this. The library instrumentation you have installed should already have created a span for you. Instead of creating a new span, get the current span and decorate it with additional attributes. More attributes on a smaller number of spans usually results in a better observability experience.

How Much Is Too Much?

With tracing and logging, people often ask how to determine the right amount of detail. Should every function be wrapped in a span? Should every line of code be logged?

These questions have no clear-cut answers. But we recommend the following pattern: unless it is a critical operation, don't add it until you need it. When starting with OpenTelemetry, don't worry about application-level instrumentation. Take a breadth-first approach, not a depth-first one.

If you're tracking down production issues, end-to-end tracing matters more than fine-grained detail. It is better to stand every service up with just the instrumentation OpenTelemetry provides and then progressively add instrumentation in specific areas when you desire additional detail. You can also focus on smaller, self-contained areas to start and then broaden your instrumentation as needed. In either case, quite a bit of the value in observability more generally is in custom instrumentation for your business logic, and other values that automatic instrumentation can't capture. With that in mind, don't get wrapped up in thinking about the "correct" amount of detail and focus instead on what you and your team need. This approach lets you ask—and answer—interesting questions. (For more on this subject, see Chapter 9.)

Layering Spans and Metrics

Metrics are good for more than just measuring how much CPU is in use in your service or how long garbage collection pauses take. Using application metrics effectively can save money and enable you to analyze long-term performance trends.

It's a good practice to create histogram metrics for your API endpoints, especially high-throughput ones. *Histograms* are a particular type of metric stream that consists of buckets, and counts that fall into those buckets. You can think of them as ways to capture distributions of values.

OpenTelemetry supports both standard, predefined histograms and *exponential bucket* histograms. The latter are extremely useful. They automatically adjust for the scale and range of the measurements you put into them. They also can be added together. This means you could run one hundred instances of an API server, all creating exponential histograms to track throughput, error rate, and latency, and then sum all the values, even if their scales and ranges differ. If you combine this with exemplars, then you can get not only highly accurate statistics about service performance, but also contextual links to traces that demonstrate performance by bucket.

Browser and Mobile Clients

The devices users interact with, such as phones, laptops, touchscreens, and cars, are critical components in our distributed systems. Browser and mobile clients often run in restrictive environments with low memory and poor network connectivity. Solving these performance problems without client telemetry is difficult. It can also be difficult to understand how changes to product features or the GUI will affect the user experience.

In observability, client telemetry is traditionally referred to as *real user monitoring* (RUM). As of this writing, RUM is under active development for browsers, iOS, and Android.

Public Gateways

When you deploy OpenTelemetry for client monitoring, remember that the OpenTelemetry Collector is not designed to be a public gateway. If your client SDKs are sending data to Collectors instead of directly to an analysis tool, consider standing up an additional proxy for use as a public gateway, configured with an appropriate security regime for your organization.

Secondary Observability Signals

You may have heard of *signals* like profiling, sessions, and events. These are specialized types of telemetry data used in techniques such as RUM and *continuous profiling* (a way to get code-level telemetry data from a running process). As of this writing, these signals are not yet stable in OpenTelemetry, but work is underway. Ultimately, OpenTelemetry is agnostic to how signals are actually used; it focuses on how to create, collect, and express them in a standardized way. This includes unifying them. RUM is an important part of understanding a distributed system, but you need to connect it to backend telemetry to really transform your observability practice.

The Complete Setup Checklist

Telemetry is incredibly important! But there are many moving pieces, and it's easy to miss something when you are first starting out. Like a pilot inspecting their airplane before takeoff, you will find it helpful to have a checklist to follow when verifying a successful installation of OpenTelemetry. Here's a simple one to get you started.

☐ **Is instrumentation available for every important library?**

HTTP, frameworks, database clients, and messaging systems should all be instrumented. Double-check that the libraries you are using are actually included on the list of available instrumentation.

☐ **Does the SDK register show providers for tracing, metrics, and logs?**

You can check that the SDK is registered correctly by executing a function that explicitly creates a span, metric, and log (or whichever signals you're using).

☐ **Is the exporter correctly installed?**

Are the protocol, endpoint, and TLS certificate options configured?

☐ **Are the correct propagators installed?**

If you do not intend to use the standard W3C tracing headers, check that traces correctly record a parent ID when the intended tracing header is included as part of an incoming HTTP request.

☐ **Is the SDK sending data to the Collector?**

In your Collector, add a `logging` exporter to every pipeline, with verbosity set to `detailed`. This will show you whether the SDK is successfully sending data to the Collector.

☐ **Is the Collector sending data to the analysis tool?**

If you have proven that the SDK is sending data to the Collector, any remaining telemetry pipeline problem is a misconfiguration between the Collector and the analysis tool.

☐ **Are the correct resources emitted?**

List all the resource attributes you expect to be present on every service and include them in your checklist. Verify that these resources are present on the traces and logs emitted from these services.

☐ **Are all traces complete?**

In the trace analysis tool, verify that the trace appears and that it contains a span for every instrumented library in every service participating in the transaction.

If *all* of the spans from a particular service are missing in a trace, then something earlier in this checklist has failed for that service.

If a trace appears to be connected and complete from end to end but is missing an expected span somewhere in the middle, then instrumentation has not been properly set up for that particular library.

☐ **Are no traces broken?**

A trace is broken when it successfully makes it to the backend but appears as multiple separate traces. This happens when a span is created without a parent span and thus creates a new trace ID.

If a trace is broken between services, check for matching CLIENT and SERVER spans in each partial trace. If one of these spans is missing, then a piece of HTTP instrumentation is missing.

If CLIENT and SERVER spans exist, check whether the client and server SDKs are both configured to use the same propagation format (such as W3C, B3, or XRAY). If they are configured correctly, inspect the HTTP request and confirm whether the tracing headers are actually present. If they are not present, the client is failing to correctly inject the propagation headers. If they are present, the server is failing to correctly extract the headers.

If everything in this checklist passes, congratulations! Your services are properly instrumented with OpenTelemetry and are ready for production.

Packaging It All Up

If you're using OpenTelemetry, you probably have multiple services as part of your application. Large distributed systems can have hundreds of different services, all of which will need to be instrumented. This may involve multiple development teams that own different parts of the system.

Regardless of how large your system is, once you have successfully instrumented one application, it's good to package everything up to make it easier to add Open-Telemetry to the rest of your applications. It's also good to write some internal documentation, explaining all the settings and setup procedures that are specific to your organization. (See Chapter 9 for more on rolling out observability.)

Setting up an application with OpenTelemetry can be tricky, because you need to learn and interact with every part of OpenTelemetry in the process. Understanding what the major components are and how they relate to each other makes it easier to verify that everything has been installed correctly and to debug any issues.

One great way to package OpenTelemetry is to add instrumentation directly to libraries and frameworks. This reduces the number of packages to install and simplifies installation in your applications. In the next chapter, we'll discuss how to do this.

Conclusion

The work required to reinstrument a large system often turns into a form of vendor lock-in—it's just too expensive and time-consuming to change everything. But the advantage of OpenTelemetry is that once it's done, it's done! You will never have to go through that process again, even if you switch analysis tools or vendors. Switching to OpenTelemetry means switching to a standard that works with *every* observability system.

CHAPTER 6

Instrumenting Libraries

The price of reliability is the pursuit of the utmost simplicity. It is a price which the very rich find most hard to pay.

—Sir Antony Hoare[1]

Internet applications are all very similar. Their code is not written in a vacuum; their developers apply a common set of tools—network protocols, databases, thread pools, HTML—to solve a specific problem. That's why we call them *applications*. The tools these applications leverage are called *libraries*, and that is what we will focus on in this chapter.

Shared libraries are those that have been widely adopted across many applications. Most shared libraries are open source, but not all: two notable proprietary shared libraries are the Cocoa (*https://oreil.ly/CdXVT*) and SwiftUI (*https://oreil.ly/FAoEo*) frameworks provided by Apple. Regardless of its license, the wide adoption of a library can create additional challenges that are not present when you're instrumenting ordinary application code. When we use the term *library* in this chapter, this type of shared library is what we mean.

OpenTelemetry is designed for library instrumentation. If you're a maintainer of one of these libraries, this chapter is for you. Even libraries that are internal to a single organization will benefit from the advice that follows. If you're just looking for best practices, you'll find those sections at the end of the chapter.

---

1 Charles Antony Richard Hoare, "1980 ACM Turing Award Lecture: The Emperor's Old Clothes," *Communications of the ACM* 24, no. 2 (February 1981): 75–83.

As a maintainer, the idea of instrumenting your own library may be a novel concept. We call this practice *native instrumentation*, and we hope to convince you that it is superior to the traditional approach, in which instrumentation is maintained by a third party. We'll also cover why high-quality library telemetry is so critical to observability and look at the barriers that maintainers face when they write instrumentation themselves.

As we did in Chapter 5, we provide a checklist of best practices to use when instrumenting libraries. We also touch on additional best practices that come with *shared services*, such as databases, load balancers, and container platforms like Kubernetes.

Beyond the actual code that goes into the library itself, native instrumentation opens the door to a wider set of practices that we believe are beneficial for library maintainers and users alike. These are new ideas, and we look forward to developing them with you as native instrumentation becomes more common.

The Importance of Libraries

The distinction between application code and libraries may seem obvious, but it has important ramifications for observability. Remember, most production problems don't originate from simple bugs in application logic: they come from large numbers of concurrent user requests to access shared resources interacting in ways that cause unexpected behavior and cascading failures that do not appear in development.

Most resource usage within most applications occurs within library code, not within application code. Application code itself rarely consumes a large amount of resources; instead, it *directs* library code to utilize resources. The problem is that application code may direct those libraries poorly. For example, it might direct an application to gather resources in serial when they could more efficiently be gathered in parallel, leading to excess latency (as shown in Figure 6-1).

Beyond making everything slower, multiple requests attempting to simultaneously read and write from the same resources can create consistency errors. A request that reads data from several independent resources may attempt to prevent inconsistent reads by trying to obtain a lock on every resource for the duration of the transaction. But this may result in deadlock when another request tries to obtain a lock on the same resources in a different order. It's true that these problems *are* bugs in the application logic, but they are induced by the fundamental nature of the shared systems those applications are attempting to access—and they manifest only in production.

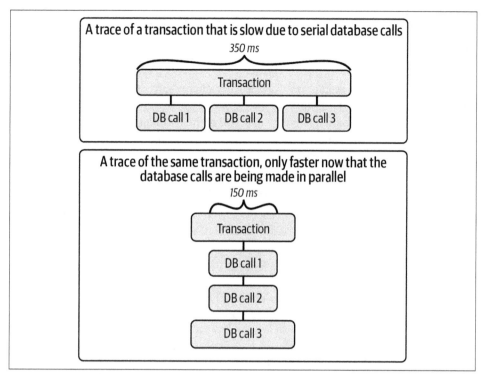

Figure 6-1. Serial database calls (top) that could be replaced by parallel calls (bottom) to significantly reduce latency

To make matters worse, production problems can compound. As overall load on a database increases, every request to that database becomes slower. Slow requests can in turn increase the chances of inconsistent reads, deadlocks, and other bugs. The deadlocks and inconsistent reads cascade into further failures, which can spread across an entire system.

When investigating all these problems, it's important to look at patterns of library usage. This puts libraries at the forefront of observability—which means that high-quality telemetry for libraries is critical.

Why Provide Native Instrumentation?

It's clear that library telemetry is critical. But why is native instrumentation important? What's wrong with just providing some hooks and letting your users write plug-ins for whatever instrumentation they would like to add—or better yet, just having the observability system dynamically insert everything with auto-instrumentation?

It turns out that writing your own instrumentation has a number of advantages for both you and your users. This section will explain these advantages in some detail.

Observability Works by Default in Native Instrumentation

Observability systems are notoriously difficult to set up, and a big part of why that's the case is the need to install and instrument plug-ins for every library.

But what if the instrumentation was already there—off by default, but instantly switched on across every library in the application the moment the user installs something to receive the data? And what if that instrumentation all used the same standards to describe common operations, like HTTP requests? This would dramatically lower the barrier for observability.

What's Wrong with Plug-Ins?

You might be wondering why you need native instrumentation when you could instead provide hooks that let someone else write the plug-ins.

Well, for one, when you delegate key features to a plug-in, you are now dependent on someone else writing and updating it. When you release a new version of your library, it won't ship with correct instrumentation; until the plug-in author notices and updates the plug-in, your users will have a degraded experience.

More subtly, plug-ins confine your instrumentation to places in which you feel comfortable allowing your users to execute arbitrary code. Plug-ins require hooks into your library's runtime, which add surface area that you will have to support in the future. Architecture improvements often change which hooks are available, which breaks plug-in compatibility. The more hooks you have, the worse your compatibility problems become.

Finally, plug-ins and hooks add a layer of indirection, which can increase overhead. Whatever data you provide will have to be converted into the format the instrumentation uses, which wastes memory.

Native Instrumentation Lets You Communicate with Your Users

Owning your library's telemetry facilitates communication. As a library maintainer, you have a relationship and a responsibility to your users. Telemetry is an important part of maintaining this relationship, and it's important to speak with your own voice. The metrics and traces you provide will power the dashboards, alerts, and firefighting tools that your users need to keep their systems running. You'll want to warn them when they misconfigure something, exceed the maximum size of a buffer, or experience a failure. You can use the telemetry you produce to communicate with your users about these issues.

One way to communicate with your users is through documentation and playbooks, and another is through dashboards and alerts.

Documentation and playbooks

When you own your observability, you have a precise schema that you can use to explain how your library works.

For example, you can use traces to describe the structure of your library. This gives new users valuable feedback and helps them visualize how they are using your library. There are many ways to use a library incorrectly—for example, performing operations serially when they could be parallelized, suboptimal configuration of caches or buffers, reinstantiating clients or objects rather than reusing them when appropriate, or unintentional mutation of data due to improper use of mutexes. If you show your users what to look for, tracing can make it easy for them to identify common "gotchas" and antipatterns.

You can also create playbooks that document the warnings and errors your library emits and explain how to fix each problem. Many libraries provide configuration options for tuning various parameters. But when should users change these settings, and how can they confirm that they've tuned them correctly? Telemetry can form the basis for these instructions.

Dashboards and alerts

Your library will also emit metrics, which should always be designed with a use case in mind. Any library that emits metrics should recommend a default set of dashboards that new users should set up when they start monitoring their application, including common performance metrics that are derived from trace data. If you have explicitly defined the exact telemetry your library emits, it will be easy to describe a default set of dashboards and alerts using the exact attribute names and values your users will need when setting them up.

All of this may sound like extra work, but it's quite valuable. If you try to add tests to a library built without them, you may discover that it was built in a way that makes it untestable. The same is true for observability: working on observability as you develop, and describing how your users should make use of that observability, will improve your library's design and architecture. Clear communication is as valuable for the speaker as it is for the listener.

Native Instrumentation Shows That You Care About Performance

Observability can also be thought of as a form of testing. In fact, it's the *only* form of testing we have available when running production systems. What are alerts if not tests? "I expect that X will not exceed Y for more than Z minutes" sure looks like a test.

But you can also use observability as a form of testing during development. Generally speaking, developers spend a lot of time testing for logical errors, but very little time testing for performance problems and resource usage. Given how many cascading production problems stem from latency, timeouts, resource contention, and unexpected behavior under load, this is worth revisiting.

As an industry, we have reached a stage at which observability needs to become a first-class citizen. Like testing, observability should be an important and informative part of the development process, not tacked on as an afterthought. And if the library maintainer is not in charge of their own observability, this can never happen.

Why Aren't Libraries Already Instrumented?

Now that you've learned how important library telemetry is, you might be surprised to discover that almost *no* libraries currently emit any telemetry at all. Library instrumentation is almost always written by someone other than the maintainer and installed after the fact. Why? Two reasons: composition and tracing.

Observability systems don't compose well. In the past, instrumentation has always been tied to a specific observability system. Picking an instrumentation library has also meant picking a client and a data format.

So what happens if you pick one observability tool and another library picks a different one? The user now has to run two completely separate observability tools. More likely, they have to rely on a third-party agent or integration to translate between your choice and their choice of tools. This is the status quo for most library authors; they emit logs, which can be translated into metrics, and rely on their users to fill in the blanks.

Even something as simple as logging errors can be problematic. Which logging library should you pick? If you have many users, there's no right answer; some of them use one logging library, and some of them use another. Most languages provide a variety of logging facades to ease this problem, but there's no truly universal solution. Even logging to `stdout` will be problematic for some users. As Figure 6-2 shows, no choice a library maintainer can make will be correct in all applications.

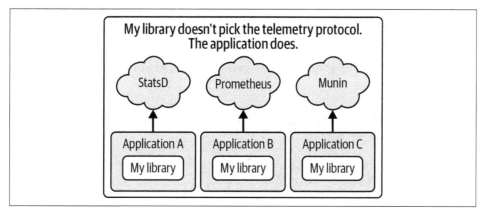

Figure 6-2. There is no right answer when different applications use different observability systems

Right out of the gate, then, library authors and maintainers are stuck, because they're not in a position to choose the observability system. The application maintainer must make this choice, since it affects the entire application.

Tracing is the real blocker for library observability. Juggling multiple logging and metrics systems would be inefficient and annoying, but possible. Where things truly fall apart is with tracing. Since tracing propagates context across library boundaries, it works only if all libraries are using the same tracing system.

A handful of languages offer logging and metrics interfaces capable of interoperating across libraries—Log4j and Micrometer are two examples for Java. But at the time of this writing, no acceptable tracing option is available for library instrumentation, except for OpenTelemetry and its predecessor, OpenTracing. So let's pivot and look at the qualities that make OpenTelemetry such a good fit for library instrumentation.

How OpenTelemetry Is Designed to Support Libraries

Instrumentation is a *cross-cutting concern*—that is, a subsystem that ends up everywhere, used by every part of the codebase. Security and exception handling are other examples of cross-cutting concerns.

Normally, sprinkling API calls everywhere would be an antipattern. Compartmentalizing functionality is a best practice in application design, as is limiting the number of places in which different libraries interact. For example, it's better to encapsulate all of the code that deals with database access in one part of the codebase. It would be alarming to see SQL calls everywhere, mixed in with HTML rendering and all kinds of other code.

But cross-cutting concerns have to interact with every part of an application, so you'll need to handle the interfaces for these software features with extreme care. In this section, we'll look at several best practices for writing cross-cutting concerns and show you how following those practices makes OpenTelemetry a good fit for library instrumentation.

OpenTelemetry Separates the Instrumentation API and the Implementation

Earlier we pointed out that while individual libraries emit library-specific telemetry, end users need to make application-wide choices for how to process and export all of that telemetry as a whole. So we have two separate concerns: writing instrumentation for a particular library, and configuring the telemetry pipeline for the entire application. Two separate people handle those concerns: the library maintainer and the application maintainer.

This separation of concerns brings us back to the architecture of OpenTelemetry, which separates the instrumentation API from the implementation for precisely this reason. The library maintainer needs an interface for writing instrumentation for the code they own, and the application maintainer needs to install and configure plug-ins and exporters and make other application-wide decisions.

Transitive dependency conflicts include incompatible versions of an API (discussed later in this section), but they don't stop there. If that API package *itself* relies on a large number of dependencies, there is a chance that those dependencies will themselves cause problems.

Splitting the API from the implementation solves this problem. The API itself has almost no dependencies. The SDK and all its dependencies are referenced only once, by the application developer during setup. This means that the app developer can resolve any dependency conflicts by choosing different plug-ins or implementations.

This pattern of loose coupling enables OpenTelemetry to solve the issue of embedding instrumentation into shared libraries that will be installed in many applications with different owners.

OTel Maintains Backward Compatibility

Separating the API from the implementation is important but not sufficient on its own. The API also needs to maintain compatibility across all the libraries that use it.

If the API were to break frequently, with new major versions published on a regular basis, compatibility would be broken. It doesn't matter if the project correctly follows semver and releases new major versions in a responsible manner. A new major version number would create a *transitive dependency conflict*, which occurs when an application depends on two libraries, and those two libraries depend on incompatible versions of a third library (Figure 6-3).

Figure 6-3. Two libraries that depend on different major versions of the API cannot be compiled into the same application

To avoid this issue, all OpenTelemetry APIs are backward compatible. In fact, backward compatibility is a strict requirement for the OpenTelemetry project. We have to assume that instrumentation, once written, may never be updated again. Thus, in OpenTelemetry stable APIs are released as v1.0, with no plans to ever release a v2.0. This ensures that any existing instrumentation will continue to work even a decade into the future.

OTel Keeps Instrumentation Off by Default

What happens to instrumentation when a library is installed in an application that doesn't use OpenTelemetry? Nothing at all. OpenTelemetry API calls are always safe; they will never throw an exception.

In native instrumentation, the OpenTelemetry API is used directly within the library code, without any kind of wrapper or indirection. Because the OpenTelemetry API has zero overhead and is off by default, library maintainers can embed OpenTelemetry instrumentation directly in their code, rather than in a plug-in or behind a wrapper that needs to be configured in order to work.

Why does this matter? Because every library requires a plug-in or a configuration change to enable instrumentation, end users have to do a lot of work to make their applications observable. They might even miss that instrumentation is available as an option!

Imagine an application that uses five libraries (pictured in Figure 6-4). Now there are five places that need configuration, and five opportunities to fail to enable the telemetry that is critical to observing the application.

With native instrumentation, no configuration is needed. As Figure 6-5 shows, when the user registers the SDK, it immediately starts receiving telemetry from all libraries. The user doesn't have to take any additional steps.

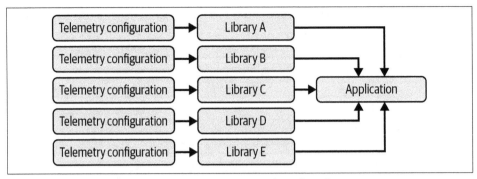

Figure 6-4. Non-native instrumentation requires a lot of configuration

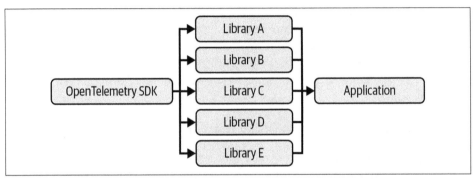

Figure 6-5. All native instrumentation is automatically enabled as soon as the SDK is installed

Shared Libraries Checklist

So what should you do when instrumenting your library? The following checklist of best practices encapsulates what we believe to be a successful approach. If you do the following, you can make your library one of the most observable and operator-friendly libraries available.

☐ **Have you enabled OpenTelemetry by default?**

It may be tempting to provide OpenTelemetry as an option that is disabled by default. This will prevent your library from automatically enabling instrumentation when the user registers their OpenTelemetry implementation. Remember, the OpenTelemetry API is off by default, activating only when the application owner turns it on. If you add a step by requiring users to configure your library to enable OpenTelemetry, they're less likely to use it.

☐ **Have you avoided wrapping the API?**

It might be tempting to wrap the OpenTelemetry API in a custom API, but the OpenTelemetry API is pluggable! If a user wants a different implementation, they can register it as an OpenTelemetry provider, enabling that implementation across all libraries that use OpenTelemetry.

☐ **Have you used existing semantic conventions?**

OpenTelemetry provides a standard schema for describing most common operations, such as HTTP requests, database calls, and message queues: the *OpenTelemetry Semantic Conventions*. Review the semantic conventions (*https://oreil.ly/9PD90*) and make sure your instrumentation uses them everywhere they apply.

☐ **Have you created new semantic conventions?**

For operations that are specific to your library, use the existing semantic conventions as a guide for writing your own. Document these conventions for your users. If your library has multiple implementations in multiple languages, consider upstreaming your conventions to OpenTelemetry so that other library maintainers can use them.

☐ **Have you imported only API packages?**

When writing instrumentation, it is sometimes possible to reference an SDK package by mistake. Make sure your library references only API packages.

☐ **Have you pinned your library to the major version number?**

To avoid creating dependency conflicts with other libraries, it is important to allow your library to take a dependency on any future version of the OpenTelemetry API, up to the next major version. For example, if your library requires an API feature added in version 1.2.0, you should require the version range `v1.2.0 < v2.0.0`.[2]

☐ **Have you provided comprehensive documentation?**

Provide documentation that describes the telemetry your library produces. In particular, make sure to describe any library-specific conventions you have created. Provide playbooks for how to correctly tune and operate your library, based on the telemetry it provides.

☐ **Have you tested performance and shared the results?**

Use the telemetry you have to create performance tests and provide the results to your users.

---

2 While OpenTelemetry doesn't plan on releasing a version 2.0, it would be bad practice to recommend taking a dependency on a new major version. So much software is so bad at backward compatibility that users have become accustomed to mistrusting any kind of update, but here, trust that minor version bumps really would be minor version bumps.

Shared Services Checklist

We've described how users can compose shared libraries into their applications, but another type of open source system deserves attention: *shared services*. These are entirely self-contained standalone applications, such as databases, proxies, and messaging systems.

When instrumenting a shared service, all of the best practices for shared libraries still apply. We recommend adding the following as well:

☐ **Have you used the OpenTelemetry config file?**

Allow users to configure the telemetry your system produces the same way they configure it for all other services: by exposing the standard OpenTelemetry configuration options and environment variables.

☐ **Are you outputting OTLP by default?**

While it's fine to include additional exporters and plug-ins, simply providing OTLP over HTTP/Proto as the default exporting option is sufficient. Users can split and transform this output downstream by using a Collector.

☐ **Have you bundled a local Collector?**

If you are providing a virtual machine or container image, consider providing a version with a local Collector installed for capturing machine metrics and additional resources.

Conclusion

If you can't write your own instrumentation, it's hard to produce telemetry. And if you can't produce telemetry, it's hard to care about performance. Putting the control—and the responsibility—into the right hands is an important part of how OpenTelemetry is helping people redesign and rethink observability.

We hope that you agree with us, and that this chapter has helped you to consider all the ways you can incorporate observability into your development practice. In five years, we'd like developers to be thinking of runtime observability as being just as important as testing. If you find this inspiring too, please join us in making this dream a reality!

CHAPTER 7

Observing Infrastructure

We build our computer systems the way we build our cities: over time, without a plan, on top of ruins.

—Ellen Ullman[1]

Despite the many advances in cloud computing, serverless, and other technologies that promise to shield programmers from having to care about where and how their programs run, we are still stymied by a basic fact: software has to run on hardware. What has changed, though, is how we interact with hardware. Rather than relying on bare syscalls, we rely heavily on increasingly sophisticated APIs and other abstractions of the underlying infrastructure that powers our software.

Infrastructure isn't limited to physical hardware either. Planet-scale cloud computing platforms offer managed services for everything from key management to caches to text-message gateways. New AI- and ML-powered services seem to crop up weekly, and new orchestration and deployment methods promise more speed and flexibility in where and how code runs.

Infrastructure is a key part of any software system, and understanding your infrastructure resources is a key part of observability. In this chapter, we'll cover infrastructure observability with OpenTelemetry and discuss how to understand and model this part of your systems.

---

1 Ellen Ullman, quoted in the introduction to *Kill It with Fire: Manage Aging Computer Systems (and Future Proof Modern Ones)* by Marianne Bellotti (Burlingame, CA: No Starch Press, 2021).

What Is Infrastructure Observability?

Just about every developer or operator has done some infrastructure *monitoring*, such as watching a system's CPU utilization, memory usage, or free disk space, or even a remote host's uptime. Monitoring is an extremely common task when working with computers. What separates infrastructure *observability* from monitoring tasks? Context. While it's useful to know how much memory a given Kubernetes node uses, that statistic tells you little about what parts of the system influence it.

Infrastructure observability is concerned with two things: infrastructure providers and infrastructure platforms. *Providers* are the actual "source" of infrastructure, such as datacenters or cloud providers. Amazon Web Services (AWS), Google Cloud Platform (GCP), and Microsoft Azure are infrastructure providers.

Platforms are higher-level abstractions over those providers that provide some sort of managed service and vary in size, complexity, and purpose. Kubernetes, which aids in container orchestration, is a type of platform. *Functions as a service (FaaS)* such as AWS Lambda, Google App Engine, and Azure Cloud Functions are serverless platforms. Platforms aren't necessarily limited to code or container runtimes either; continuous integration and continuous delivery (CI/CD) platforms, such as Jenkins, are a type of infrastructure platform.

Incorporating infrastructure observability into your overall observability profile can be challenging. This is because infrastructure resources are most often shared—many requests can use the same unit of infrastructure at the same time, and figuring out the correlation between infrastructure and service state is difficult. Even if you do have the ability to perform this correlation, is the data that you get useful? Your infrastructure needs to be designed in such a way that you can act on these insights.

We can create a simple taxonomy of "what matters" when it comes to observability. In short:

- Can you establish context (either hard or soft) between specific infrastructure and application signals?
- Does understanding these systems through observability help you achieve specific business/technical goals?

If the answer to both of these questions is no, then you probably don't need to incorporate that infrastructure signal into your observability framework. That doesn't mean you don't want—or need—to monitor that infrastructure! It just means you'll need to use different tools, practices, and strategies for that monitoring than you would use for observability.

Let's step through providers and platforms with an eye to these questions and discuss what telemetry signals we need and how OpenTelemetry can help us acquire them. First, we'll discuss using OpenTelemetry to collect signals from cloud infrastructure, such as virtual machines or API gateways. After that, we'll look deeper into observability strategies for Kubernetes, serverless, and event-driven architectures.

Observing Cloud Providers

Cloud providers offer a fire hose of telemetry data. Your responsibility is to retrieve and store only what's most relevant. So how do you know what infrastructure data is relevant?

The most important question you need to answer is "What telemetry data is valuable to my observability?" Consider a single EC2 instance on AWS. Hundreds of metrics could be available from a single instance, with dozens of dimensions: health checks, CPU utilization, bytes written to disk, network traffic in and out, CPU credits consumed, and so on. A Java service running on that instance would expose many more metrics: statistics around garbage collection, thread count, memory consumption, and more. This instance and service would also create system logs, kernel logs, access logs, JVM runtime logs, and more.

We can't really provide a completely authoritative guide to managing telemetry from each service on each cloud. Instead, let's look at what kinds of services are common in cloud native architectures and then examine some solutions for managing those signals through OpenTelemetry.

We can broadly categorize the services available through cloud providers into two groups. The first is *bare infrastructure*, which includes on-demand and scalable services that provide compute, storage, networking, and so forth: on-demand virtual machines, blob storage, API gateways, or managed databases. The second is *managed services*—these can be on-demand Kubernetes clusters, machine learning, stream processors, or serverless platforms.

In a traditional datacenter, you'd be responsible for aggregating metrics and logs. Cloud providers usually perform this step for you via services such as AWS Cloud-Watch, but you're also free to collect them. You can do so through preexisting or custom receivers in OpenTelemetry.

You've learned that OpenTelemetry is built on the hard context provided by tracing. You've also learned that profiling transactions that offer meaningful opportunities for performance improvement is an important part of observability. With that in mind, let's take a deeper dive into integrating cloud-infrastructure metrics and logs into your OpenTelemetry strategy.

Collecting Cloud Metrics and Logs

If you're building in the cloud, then you're almost certainly already collecting metrics and logs. Each cloud provider offers various services and agents that emit system monitoring data and log contents to its own (or third-party) monitoring services. The question you need to answer when you come calling with OpenTelemetry is, *what signals are valuable to observability?* Many, but not all, of the signals emitted from your existing infrastructure are useful for integration into your observability strategy. You can think of cloud telemetry as an "iceberg," as illustrated in Figure 7-1. While OpenTelemetry is capable of collecting all of these signals, you should think about how they fit into your overall monitoring posture.

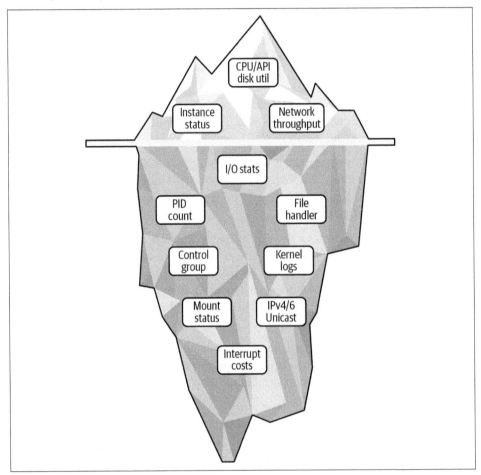

Figure 7-1. The cloud telemetry iceberg

Take instance status. "Is the computer running or not?" may seem to be an absolutely crucial piece of data to track, but in a distributed system, a single virtual machine being up or down doesn't tell you much. And you wouldn't rely on instance availability metrics alone to solve a problem, as it would be a single data point. While it can be a useful event to keep track of, looking at *just* this data wouldn't tell you a lot about the overall state of the system. A well-architected distributed system should be fairly resilient to a single node being offline, for example.

However, when you look at this event as part of an observability system, it becomes more useful. If you can correlate an instance being offline to an improperly routed request through an API gateway or load balancer, you can use that to diagnose poor performance for user requests. If those metrics or traces that use those signals feed into SLOs, that data becomes a valuable part of your overall business and reliability engineering posture. Even if a single signal might not appear valuable in isolation, its value needs to be considered as part of an overall observability strategy.

To this end, you do need to consider what signals are important to collect and how to use them. Doing so requires you to adopt a few foundational principles:

- Use semantic conventions to build soft context between metric signals and application telemetry. Ensure that metadata emitted from service code and infrastructure uses the same keys and values.

- You don't have to reinvent the wheel: leverage existing integrations and formats where possible. The OpenTelemetry Collector has a large plug-in ecosystem that allows you to convert existing telemetry from many sources into OpenTelemetry Protocol (OTLP).

- Be purposeful with your data! You should really think about how you're collecting your metrics and logs, what you actually need, and how long you need to keep it. We've talked to developers who spent $10 or less on compute resources for a cloud job that generated over $150 in logging costs!

Your main tool for capturing or transforming cloud metric and log data will be the OpenTelemetry Collector (*https://opentelemetry.io/docs/collector*). You can deploy it in a variety of ways—you could install it as a system service on Linux or Windows hosts to directly scrape metrics, or you could deploy multiple Collectors to scrape remote metrics endpoints. A complete discussion of installation and configuration options is outside the scope of this book, but in this section we'll go through some configuration and usage best practices.

While you can easily pull a Docker container or prebuilt binary image of the Collector, production deployments should rely on the Collector Builder (*https://oreil.ly/UOy49*). This utility allows you to generate a custom build with the specific receivers, exporters, and processors you need built in. You may also run into problems that are best solved by adding a custom module to the Collector—using the builder makes this easier, so it's a good habit to get into.

When it comes to attributes, err on the side of "too many" early in your metric pipeline. It's easier to throw away data you don't need before it gets sent for analysis than to add in data that doesn't exist. Adding a new dimension can cause a *cardinality explosion*, or a dramatic increase in the number of time series a metric database needs to store, but you can control this by allow-listing metrics later in the pipeline.

Push Versus Pull

OpenTelemetry is generally agnostic to push versus pull metrics (a system in which metrics are transmitted from hosts to central servers versus one in which a central server fetches metrics from well-known paths), but it's important to note that OTLP has no concept of pull-based metrics. If you choose to use OTLP, then your metrics will be pushed.

As OpenTelemetry adoption increases, more vendors are creating native offerings to export metric data in OTLP format. We go into more detail about this shortly, so read on!

You always have the option to use the Collector to directly produce and transmit metrics and log data from virtual machines, containers, and so forth. There are many out-of-the-box integrations for this, such as the `hostmetrics` receiver.

To avoid laborious remapping (see the next subsection for more on this), try to find a handful of attributes that you'd like to share across preexisting metrics and logs and add them to your trace and application metric signals, rather than the other way around. If you're starting from scratch, consider building around OpenTelemetry from the start by using the Collector and the SDK to capture system and process telemetry.

One of the more popular deployment architecture implementations is illustrated in Figure 7-2. Here, Collectors act as a "gateway," unifying telemetry coming from multiple aggregators or technologies. Note that not all components in the Collector are stateless; log processing and transformation are, but Prometheus scrapers are not, for example. Figure 7-3 demonstrates a more advanced version of the architecture with an application service and database, wherein each component has independent Collectors that can scale horizontally per signal type.

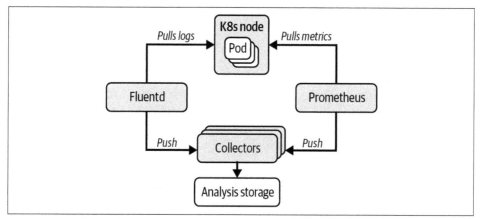

Figure 7-2. A "gateway" deployment of the Collector monitoring a Kubernetes node, where Prometheus and FluentD scrape metrics and logs and then send them to external Collectors that process any signal

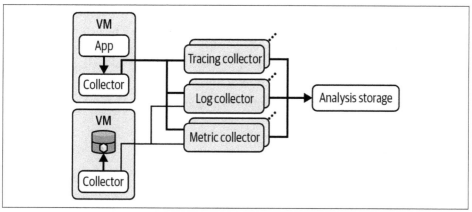

Figure 7-3. A "gateway" deployment of the Collector, much like Figure 7-2, but instead of all telemetry being sent to the same pool of collectors, different signal types are emitted to specialized pools of collectors

Metamonitoring

Metamonitoring—that is, monitoring your Collector's performance—is important as well. The Collector exposes a handful of metrics, such as `otelcol_processor _refused_spans` and `otelcol_processor_refused_metric_points` (supplied by the Memory Ballast extension[2]). These metrics will tell you if the limiter is causing the Collector to refuse new data. If so, you should scale up. Similarly, calculating the difference between the `queue_size` and `queue_capacity` metrics will let you know when the receiving service is busy.

Here are some rough rules to keep in mind when planning for Collector capacity:

- Experiment per host or per workload to determine the correct size of the ballast (a chunk of memory preallocated to the heap) for each type of Collector. Stress tests can be a good way to figure out an upper bound.
- For scraped metrics, avoid *scrape collisions* (when the next scrape is scheduled to start before the current one has completed).
- You don't have to do all of your transformations immediately; heavier processing can be moved to later stages of your pipeline. This can reduce how much memory and compute the Collector uses, which is especially valuable for Collectors running alongside a process on a VM or host.
- It's better to overprovision a little than to lose telemetry!

Wait, What Ballast?

By the time you read this, the ballast extension may have been deprecated (see https://oreil.ly/aAhsP for details) in favor of tweaks to the `GOMEMLIMIT` and `GOGC` environment variables. Make sure you reference the OpenTelemetry documentation (*https://openteleme try.io/docs/*) for the latest guidance and features of all components.

---

2 See Ross Engers's blog post "Go Memory Ballast" (*https://oreil.ly/wWFPq*) for more information about the Golang memory ballast and how Go's concurrent garbage collection affects performance.

Collectors in Containers

Many OpenTelemetry users deploy Collectors in containers, as part of Kubernetes or some other container orchestrator. Inside a container, a good rule is to use factors of 2 for memory limits and ballast. For example, set a ballast of 40% of container memory, and then a limit of 80%. This improves performance by reducing churn, as memory is cleaned up through preallocating memory to the heap, and it allows the Collector to signal producers to back off their telemetry production without crashing or restarting due to running out of memory.

Observing Platforms

Cloud native applications are often built not for virtual machines or physical hardware but for managed platforms that provide powerful, flexible abstractions over compute, memory, and data. OpenTelemetry offers some unique strategies to aid in collecting telemetry data from these platforms, and it's worth your time to familiarize yourself with them.

Kubernetes Platforms

Broadly, OpenTelemetry integrates into the Kubernetes ecosystem in two ways: through tooling to monitor and profile applications running on Kubernetes clusters, and through telemetry data about what Kubernetes components themselves are doing. Often, cloud native applications designed for Kubernetes will interact with the Kubernetes API, which makes both types of data extremely useful in investigating performance problems, deployment issues, scaling difficulties, or other production incidents.

In both cases, the OpenTelemetry Operator (*https://oreil.ly/_5TcG*) for Kubernetes allows you to manage Collector instances and automatic instrumentation of workloads running in pods.

Kubernetes telemetry

Kubernetes offers a wide variety of events, metrics, and logs to aid in managing clusters. Recent releases have also begun to add tracing (*https://oreil.ly/oRSoU*) for components such as the Kubelet and API Server. The OpenTelemetry Collector can ingest these signals, process them, and send them to analysis tools.

Depending on the size, scale, and complexity of your cluster, you could create separate Collector deployments to handle logging, metrics, and traces from system and application components independently. The Operator includes a service discovery mechanism called the Target Allocator (TA) (*https://oreil.ly/5bq8k*) that allows collectors to discover and scrape Prometheus endpoints and evenly distributes those scrape jobs across multiple collectors.

You do have another option. Three receivers are available to listen for cluster metrics and log: the k8sclusterreceiver (*https://oreil.ly/0c__c*), the k8seventsreceiver (*https://oreil.ly/Uhqoi*), and the k8sobjectsreceiver (*https://oreil.ly/wbD7b*). The kubeletstats-receiver (*https://oreil.ly/ys_GJ*) can also pull pod-level metrics. While these receivers aren't mutually exclusive with the TA-based approach of the Operator, you should pick one or the other. In the future, we expect the community to reach consensus on a single receiver approach, but as of this writing there are unknown gaps.

What's the Deal with Kubernetes Receivers?

The OpenTelemetry community generally agrees that the best method to monitor a cluster is via receivers. However, many Kubernetes-based applications use Prometheus by convention, and the kube-state-metrics and node exporter plug-ins for Prometheus are widely adopted in existing installs. If you need something that can work with existing applications and clusters, then the Operator Target Allocator is a good choice, but if you're doing a pure greenfield deployment of Kubernetes and OpenTelemetry, the receivers might work better. You may find gaps between what is collected by the Collector receivers and what is collected by Prometheus. If you'd like to get hands-on, we've provided an example based purely on OpenTelemetry logs and the metrics Collector in the book's GitHub repository.

Kubernetes applications

OpenTelemetry doesn't care where your applications run, but Kubernetes offers a wealth of metadata that is extremely valuable if you're building OpenTelemetry-based instrumentation. If that's you, most of the advice in Chapter 5 will apply, but there are some extra benefits that existing applications running in a Kubernetes cluster can take advantage of when paired with the Operator.

As mentioned, the Target Allocator allows for discovery of things to monitor in the cluster itself. The Operator also provides a custom resource for instrumentation (*https://oreil.ly/i2OPg*) that lets you inject an OpenTelemetry automatic instrumentation package into a pod. Such packages can then add instrumentation for tracing, metrics, or logs (depending on their functionality) to existing application code. You can generally use only one form of automatic instrumentation at a time, though—and proprietary instrumentation agents will conflict with OpenTelemetry ones.

A few production deployment tips for your Collector architecture:

- Use sidecar Collectors in each pod as the first stop for your telemetry. Flushing telemetry out of the process and pod and into a sidecar can ease development and deployment, because it reduces memory pressure on your business services. It also allows for cleaner shutdowns of a pod during migrations or evictions, since the process isn't potentially waiting on busy telemetry endpoints.

- Split out Collectors by signal type, so they can scale independently. You could also create pools per application, or even per service, based on your usage patterns. Log, trace, and metric processing all have different resource-consumption profiles and constraints.

- We suggest cleanly separating concerns between telemetry creation and telemetry configuration. For example, perform redaction and sampling on Collectors rather than in process. Placing hardcoded configuration in your process makes it harder to adjust things in production without redeploying services, whereas tweaking Collector configurations is often much easier.

Serverless Platforms

Serverless platforms such as AWS Lambda and Azure Cloud Functions have gained significant popularity, but they introduce observability challenges. Developers love their ease of use and opinionated structures, but their on-demand, ephemeral nature means you'll need specialized tooling to get accurate telemetry.

In addition to your standard application telemetry, serverless observability adds a few more things to pay attention to:

Invocation time
How long does the function run for?

Resource usage
How much memory and compute does the function use?

Cold start time
How long does the function take to start up when it hasn't been used recently?

These metrics should be available from your serverless provider, but how do you get the application telemetry itself? Tools like the OpenTelemetry Lambda Layer (*https:// oreil.ly/T06_m*) offer a convenient way to capture traces and metrics from AWS Lambda invocations, although you should be aware that they incur a performance overhead.

If you can't use the Lambda Layer, ensure that your function waits on the export of telemetry data, and be sure to stop recording spans or measurements before handing control back to the function invocation library. Try to precompute strings or complex attribute values that won't change from invocation to invocation, so that they can be cached. And to avoid having telemetry queued up and waiting for export, place a Collector "close" to them that's dedicated to receiving telemetry from your functions.

Ultimately, your strategy for observing your serverless infrastructure depends on what role functions play in your application architecture. You may be able to skip directly tracing Lambda invocations (or simply pass headers through them) and link a Lambda to its calling service through attributes or span events. Then you can use Lambda service logs to pinpoint specific executions and get more details about failures or performance anomalies. If you have a complex, asynchronous workflow built on top of Lambda or other serverless platforms, you'll probably be interested in more detailed information about the structures of requests themselves; we'll talk more about that in the next section.

Queues, Service Buses, and Other Async Workflows

Many modern applications are written to take advantage of event- and queue-based platforms such as Apache Kafka. In general, the architecture of these applications revolves around services that publish and subscribe to topics on a queue. This raises several interesting challenges for observability. Tracing these transactions can be less useful than in "traditional" request/response architectures, since it's often less clear when a given transaction *ends*. You'll thus need to make quite a few decisions about your observability goals, what you want to optimize, and what you're capable of optimizing.

Consider a bank loan. From the business perspective, this transaction starts when a customer fills out a loan application and ends when their payment is disbursed. This flow can be modeled logically, but the technical mechanics of this workflow interfere with the model. In Figure 7-4, we've illustrated several services, along with a queue, that all operate on the transaction. While the business flow is fairly straightforward, the technical flow needs to encompass permutations and gaps that are anything but.

It can be helpful to draw similar diagrams of your system architecture to determine whether you're in this situation. Do you have many services acting on a single record? Do those services require human intervention to proceed? Does your workflow start and end at the same place? If your workflow diagram looks less like a tree and more like a "tree of trees," then you probably have an asynchronous workflow.

Another way to make this determination is to ask yourself what kind of indicators you're interested in tracking. Do you want to know how many steps were completed in a workflow or the median time it took for a certain step to run? Are you interested in how long it took for a service to process a record and for that record to be handled? If so, you'll need to be creative.

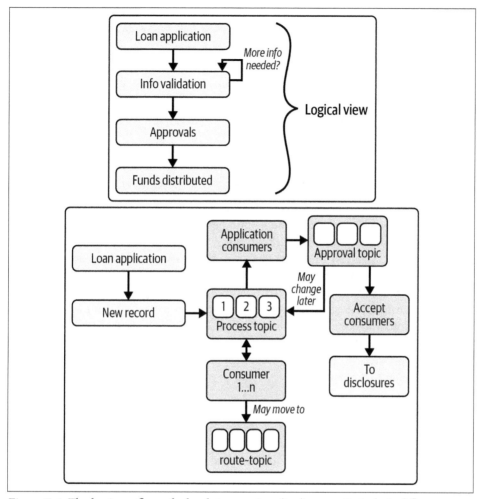

Figure 7-4. The business flow of a bank transaction (top) versus its technical flow (bottom)

Instead of thinking of any highly async workflow as a single trace, think of it as many subtraces, linked to an origin either by a custom correlation ID (a unique attribute that you ensure is on each parent span in a set of traces, usually propagated through baggage) or a shared trace ID propagated through span links. A custom correlation ID is what it sounds like: a unique attribute that you ensure is on each parent span in a set of traces, usually propagated through baggage. *Span links (https://oreil.ly/JcWS4)* allow you to create a causal relationship between spans that don't have an explicit parent-child relationship. The advantage of using links in this way is that you can calculate interesting things, such as the amount of time that work was waiting on a queue to be serviced.

In our bank loan example, you could consider the initial trace (where the transaction was created and placed on the queue) as the "primary" trace and have the terminal span of each trace link to the next root span. This requires you to have services treat the incoming span context from the message as a link, not a continuation, and start a new trace while linking to the old one. Since this relationship is initiated from the new trace, not the old one, you will need an analysis tool capable of discovering these relationships in reverse—that is, finding all traces that link together and then re-creating the journey from the end to the beginning. This type of correlation is challenging to create generalized tools for, which is why there's a lack of them; however, support for these sorts of visualizations and discovery of span links is improving. (See Appendix B for links to resources on observability frontends.)

Not all subtraces in an asynchronous transaction are equally useful. Careful use of Collector filters and samplers can be helpful here, especially if you know what kinds of questions you're interested in asking. Since the Collector allows you to convert spans to metrics, you can filter out specific subtraces and turn them into counts or histograms. If you've linked the traces together, then you can also pull in the parent trace ID as an attribute to be placed on the metrics. Imagine you have some sort of fan-out/fan-in work, such as a search or batch processing job: you could turn all child spans into a histogram, bucketed by how long it took for that particular job to complete, and then drop the child spans entirely. This would allow you to preserve the root span (and any subsequent child spans) while maintaining accurate counts and latency about its related work.

Conclusion

Infrastructure observability benefits you most when you have a clear and concise idea about your goals before you begin to implement it. Application and service observability are, strictly speaking, fairly easy in comparison. In general, instrumentation strategies for application observability don't necessarily apply to virtual machines, managed databases, or event-driven architectures using serverless technology. If there's one thing you should take away from this chapter, it's that your infrastructure observability strategy needs to be driven by your overall observability goals and aligned to organizational incentives for using the observability data your system generates. "Starting at the end" in this case will allow you to focus on what's important and what your team can actually use.

CHAPTER 8

Designing Telemetry Pipelines

I have always found that plans are useless, but planning is indispensable.
—President Dwight D. Eisenhower[1]

In the previous chapters, we have focused on managing the components that emit telemetry: applications, libraries, services, and infrastructure. Let's pivot now to managing the telemetry itself, once you have it. Collecting and processing telemetry from every single application, service, and infrastructure component is a sustained, high-throughput operation. Like any other significant component in a distributed system, it takes careful planning to design a telemetry pipeline that always makes sufficient resources available while also minimizing costs.

When telemetry is dropped, you lose observability. Because the volume of telemetry emitted by a system is directly proportional to the load on the system, operators need a clear playbook for scaling the telemetry pipeline in response to sudden traffic spikes and changes in application behavior.

If you plan on operating a telemetry pipeline, this chapter is for you. We discuss the most common telemetry pipelines you will want to adopt as your system grows. We also discuss the various kinds of processing you may want your telemetry pipeline to perform. At the end of the chapter, we focus specifically on managing Collectors within Kubernetes.

---

1 Quoted in Richard M. Nixon, *Six Crises* (Garden City, NY: Doubleday, 1962).

Common Topologies

Occasionally, a system is simple enough or new enough that no telemetry management needs to occur. But as systems grow in complexity and size, this rarely remains the case. As the system scales in size and traffic, you can add additional pieces to the telemetry pipeline to manage the load. Using the Collector as our primary component, we'll start with the simplest setup and progressively add additional Collectors to perform different roles.

No Collector

Like any program, the Collector consumes resources and requires management. But it's an optional component; if it's not providing any value, you don't have to run it. You can always add Collectors later if the need arises.

If the telemetry being emitted requires little to no processing, it may make sense to connect the SDKs directly to the backend, without a Collector. Figure 8-1 illustrates this simple setup.

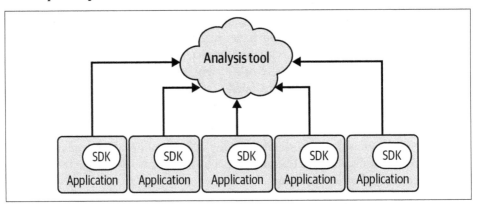

Figure 8-1. Applications send telemetry directly to the analysis tool being used

The only things missing from this setup are host metrics, such as RAM, CPU, network, and system load. In general, it is inadvisable to collect host metrics via an application. Doing so consumes application resources, and many application runtimes have difficulty reporting these metrics correctly. So, to make this simple setup work, have your host metrics reported through other channels. For example, your cloud provider may automatically collect them.

This lack of host metrics leads to the second setup: running a local Collector. This is actually a better starting point for most systems.

Local Collector

Running a local Collector on the same machine as your application has a number of benefits. Host metrics can be difficult to collect effectively from within application runtimes, so observing the host machine is the most common reason to run a local Collector. Figure 8-2 illustrates this setup.

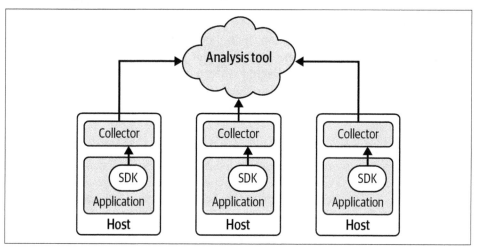

Figure 8-2. Applications send telemetry to a local Collector, which also collects host metrics

Besides collecting metrics, additional advantages to running a local Collector include the following:

Gathering environment resources

Environment resources are attributes critical for describing where telemetry originates from. You can often obtain them from your cloud provider, Kubernetes, and other sources of infrastructure. While these resources are very valuable, obtaining them often requires API or system calls. This process takes time, and in some cases API calls may require retries or fail entirely. This can lead to a delay in application startup. If you delegate this resource gathering to a local Collector, you'll free up an application to start immediately.

Avoiding data loss from crashes

Telemetry is usually exported in batches. This is efficient, but it leads to a problem—if an application crashes, any telemetry not yet exported will be lost. When exporting data to a remote receiver, you can use larger batch sizes to make transmission more efficient. But if the application crashes, you lose an even larger batch of telemetry. Considering how important the logs are when you're investigating a crash, this can be a real problem!

The solution is to set the export batch sizes and time windows on your application to be very small, so that data is evacuated quickly from the application to a local Collector. Because the Collector is on the same host, this is a fast and reliable place to send the data. Then you can configure the local Collector to batch data more appropriately for sending to a remote destination. It's a win-win situation.

As time goes on and your telemetry pipeline becomes more advanced, it tends to do more processing, filtering, and sampling. In general, the Collector is more robust and efficient at performing these operations than the individual language SDKs. But there are other reasons to separate these workloads out of the SDK and into a Collector. Most telemetry management—managing where your telemetry data is going, what format it needs to be in, and what processing needs to happen—is not specific to individual applications. Instead, it needs to be normalized across all services in the entire deployment.

Mixing telemetry configuration with application configuration can be messy. For one, it means you have to restart your applications every time there's a telemetry configuration change. It also makes coordinating telemetry changes across the fleet more difficult, since application configuration is delegated to individual teams.

In large organizations, an observability or infrastructure team usually manages telemetry configuration options. But even when organizations take a DevOps approach and have no centralized team, it's better to treat telemetry as a separate service—which is much easier to do when it is centered around the Collector.

Teams can work together to build up a shared knowledge base, including deployment strategies and tooling for Collector management. Ideally, you can design the deployment of your local Collector to avoid having to redeploy all applications running on the same machine. But even when Collector deployment is tied to application deployment, using a centralized repository makes it easy for teams to deploy the most up-to-date version of the Collector, with the correct configuration settings.

Once you've set up a local Collector, SDK configuration becomes much simpler and more stable. You can use the default configuration of OpenTelemetry Protocol (OTLP) over HTTP sent to the standard local Collector address, without any additional exporters or plug-ins. The only custom configuration should be lowering the batch size and export timeout, as mentioned previously.

Finally, you can package your organization's default SDK setup as a library and add it to your shared knowledge base. This turns your OpenTelemetry setup into a one-line operation that you can simply copy and paste into every application. This shared package also ensures that every application stays up-to-date with your latest version of OpenTelemetry.

Collector Pools

Running with local Collectors is a sufficient starting point for many organizations. However, for systems operating at large scales, adding several Collector pools to the pipeline becomes an attractive option. A *Collector pool* is a set of Collectors, each running on its own machine, that uses a load balancer to manage and distribute traffic. Figure 8-3 illustrates this setup.

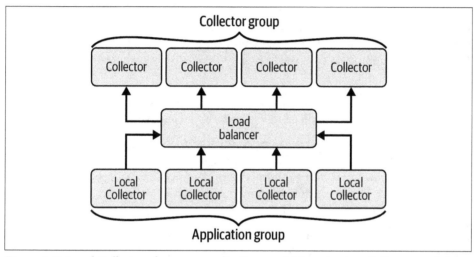

Figure 8-3. Local Collectors for every application send telemetry to a Collector pool for additional processing and buffering

Running a Collector pool has advantages. First, it means you can use load balancing to handle *backpressure*, which occurs when a producer begins to send data faster than a consumer can receive it. Applications don't produce telemetry in a steady stream. Depending on their traffic levels and design, applications sometimes begin emitting unexpectedly high volumes of telemetry. If these bursts produce telemetry faster than the analysis tool can consume it, the buffer in the Local Collector may fill to the point that it must begin dropping data to avoid running out of memory.

A Collector pool lets you add additional memory to your telemetry pipeline. The load balancer helps smooth out the spikes in telemetry caused by bursts of traffic, spreading the data evenly across the Collectors to maximize available memory. Because OTLP is stateless, this type of distributed memory buffer is simple to deploy, manage, and scale. (See "Buffering and Backpressure" on page 122 for more details.)

Resource management

Processing telemetry consumes resources. Holding telemetry requires memory, and transforming telemetry requires CPU cycles. When a local Collector is using these resources, they are no longer available to the application running on the same machine.

The local Collector has two primary purposes: allowing the application to evacuate the telemetry it produces quickly, and gathering host metrics. Any additional processing outside of these two tasks can be handed off to the Collector pool. Because these Collectors are running on their own machines, they do not compete with applications for available resources.

Collector pools are load balanced, making the resource consumption for every Collector fairly uniform and predictable. This has two advantages.

First, you can accurately match the specs on the machines requisitioned for these Collectors to the resources the Collectors are configured to consume. This allows them to run on machines with a minimal amount of headroom, ensuring there are no wasted resources. This is much harder to do with a Local Collector, which must share resources with applications of all different shapes and sizes.

Second, over time, you can analyze the average throughput for each Collector in a pool and use this information to scale the size of the pool, so that it provides the throughput needed to consume all of the telemetry the system produces.

Deployment and configuration

While running a local Collector helps separate concerns between the telemetry pipeline and the application, the fact that local Collectors must run on the same host as the application means that they are still entangled. Collector pools are completely independent, so an infrastructure team can manage them without needing to coordinate deployments with individual application teams every time they want to make a change.

OpAMP and the Future

OpenTelemetry is currently developing a protocol for managing Collectors via a control plane. The Open Agent Management Protocol (OpAMP) (*https://git hub.com/open-telemetry/opamp-spec/blob/main/specification.md*) will make it much easier to roll out configuration changes and new Collector binaries across the Collector fleet, independent of application management. It also will allow Collectors to report load and health metrics.

This approach will make it much easier for infrastructure teams to manage Collectors without having to bother the application teams. Even better, you will be able to control Collector management with the analysis tool to which the Collectors are sending information. This will allow you to tightly couple the configurations of the Collector and the analysis tool. As you change how you use the data in the analysis tool, the Collector pipelines can be automatically updated to match.

This tight coupling is especially important when managing sampling. You can't make sampling decisions independently from how the telemetry is being analyzed. Every form of analysis has an optimal sampling configuration that provides maximum value with minimal data—and this optimal configuration is notoriously difficult for humans to figure out. Allowing the analysis tool to control sampling paves the way for nuanced, safe, and precise sampling configurations, far beyond what you could manage on your own.

At the time of this writing, OpAMP is not ready for production. But we encourage you to follow the development of this protocol and make use of it once it becomes available.

Gateways and specialized workloads

In most cases, even if some applications push telemetry via OTLP and other applications pull metrics via Prometheus scraping, it is fine to have a single Collector configuration that does both.

However, as your pipeline continues to grow in size and complexity, adding specialized Collector pools can have advantages. These pools can then be connected together as needed to make pipelines that on the one hand are more complicated, but on the other hand are easier to maintain and observe. Figure 8-4 shows how a specialized pipeline might look.

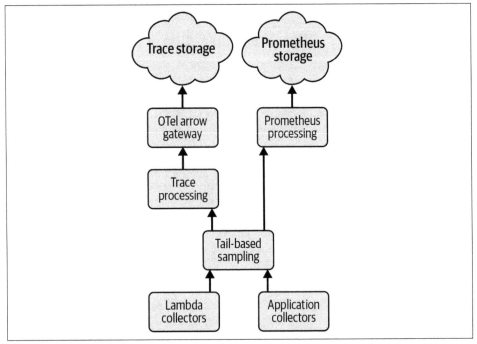

Figure 8-4. A pipeline consisting of an egress gateway and several workload-specific Collector pools

Here are some reasons you might want to create specialized Collector pools:

Reducing the size of the Collector binary

Normally, size is not an issue. But in some environments, such as FaaS, the time and cost involved in downloading a large binary can become problematic. In these cases, you might need to create a stripped-down build of the Collector with the minimal set of plug-ins needed for that particular environment, such as the OpenTelemetry Lambda Layer (*https://github.com/open-telemetry/opentelemetry-lambda*).

Reducing resource consumption

In some cases, two pipeline tasks can utilize machine resources very differently. Having the same Collector pools perform both tasks can lead to unpredictable resource consumption, requiring significantly more headroom than if the two tasks were separated onto different machines.

In these cases, it may make sense to create separate Collector pools for each task—especially if only a subset of telemetry requires one of the tasks. In each case, weigh the network cost of having separate pools against the savings gained in machine provisioning. Obviously, this separation of concerns is worthwhile only when the system is so large that the savings would be significant.

Tail-based sampling

In general, tail sampling requires all spans that make up a trace to be completed in order to make a sampling decision. The current design of the Collector's tail sampling algorithm requires that all spans for a given trace end up on the same instance in order to make the decision. This necessitates a gateway pool using a Collector with the load balancing exporter to make sure that spans go to the correct instance, and then a separate pool that performs the sampling process itself.

Keep in mind that the resource requirements for tail sampling can be very high based on span throughput, attribute count, and sampling window. The defaults for this processor assume a 30-second window of time and a max of 50,000 spans in memory at any given time. This may sound like a lot, but highly verbose traces or complex systems can easily dwarf it. We've seen production traces in the hundreds of thousands of spans for a single trace, on operations that can take many minutes to succeed or fail. We'll discuss sampling in more detail in the next section.

Backend-specific workloads

Not all telemetry requires the same processing. If, for example, you are using Prometheus for metrics and Jaeger for traces, the traces and metrics are being sent to different backends. Any Prometheus-specific Collector plug-ins for processing and managing metrics could be moved to a Collector pool that runs after metrics and traces have been separated, and right before the metrics are sent to Prometheus. This would help prevent traces from getting caught in backpressure or otherwise contending for resources with a workload that does not apply to them.

Reducing egress costs

Most cloud providers charge for network egress, and high volumes of telemetry can make these costs significant. Given that most analysis tools run in a separate network zone from the applications they monitor, high egress costs are common with large systems.

When egressing large amounts of telemetry over long periods of time, we recommend using a specialized protocol to compress the data, beyond the GZip compression of OTLP. The OTel Arrow protocol (*https://oreil.ly/otel*), in beta as we write this, is one example. Given the savings involved, we expect plenty of vendor and OSS support for OTel Arrow once it reaches stability.

Isn't OTel Arrow Better?

You might be wondering: if OTel Arrow is so efficient, why not use it *everywhere*, instead of OTLP? There are two reasons. First, to get to high levels of compression, OTel Arrow requires sustained transmission of large amounts of data. Second, OTel Arrow is a stateful protocol. For these reasons, it does not perform well with load balancers, Collector pools, or applications that send relatively small amounts of data. It's a specialized protocol designed specifically for high-throughput gateways egressing large volumes of data over a stable connection.

Pipeline Operations

Every system needs to evolve, and telemetry is no exception. While modifying your telemetry by hand-tuning each and every piece of instrumentation might be the ideal solution, it isn't often feasible. Using a pipeline of Collectors to apply changes to telemetry data and protocols is a key part of making adjustments to your observability system without creating downtime or observability blackouts. In this section, we'll review the types of operations available to you when using a Collector.

Filtering and Sampling

The first step of any pipeline should be to remove anything that you absolutely don't want. You can use filters to completely drop specific log messages, spans, or metric instruments from your pipeline. In OpenTelemetry, filters are implemented as processors, but how you use them varies slightly based on telemetry type and where they are (in the SDK or in the Collector).

The first thing to know is that while filtering and sampling both remove data, they work differently and are used to obtain different results. *Filtering* is the process of completely removing specific types of data, based on a set of rules. *Sampling* is the process of identifying a statistically representative subset of data and removing the rest.

For example, many microservice architectures expose a health-check endpoint (such as /health or /healthz) that an external monitoring script or hook checks periodically. Emitting traces for health checks is usually not very valuable, so this is an easy one to filter out—operators are never going to set alerts based on these endpoints or care about measuring their latency. It makes sense to reduce noise and lower costs by filtering out the traces for these health checks early in the telemetry pipeline.

Filtering Out the Noise

Noisy health checks are such a common nuisance that there are predefined processors for filtering based on the attributes commonly associated with health checks and synthetic monitoring. For an example of how to set up these filters, see the OpenTelemetry Demo Load Generator (*https://oreil.ly/R9ee4*).

In other cases, a system may have an operation that is valuable to monitor but also extremely common—for example, the GET request for the home page of a website. If the volume of requests is high enough, even rare outlier events become common enough that they will be picked up in a statistical sampling. You can achieve significant savings with little loss to observability by only transmitting sampling requests such as these.

You can also filter based on allow lists. In this method, instead of writing a filter that removes certain spans, you write one that allows only spans with specific names or attributes to pass through.

You can implement most filtering strategies in both the SDK and the Collector. In general, handling this processing at the Collector is a better idea than handling it at the SDK—it creates a clean separation of concerns between developers and platform engineers or SREs, and you can customize your pipeline without code redeployments. If you're wrapping the SDK or distributing it as part of an internal observability framework, however, then it can make sense to do "first-pass" filtering at the code level. You'll consume fewer resources and reduce network overhead if spans that aren't going to be collected never get created.

Sampling differs from filtering in that its goal is to reduce the overall data volume the pipeline must process. Sampling, like filtering, should happen early in the pipeline to avoid wasting time processing telemetry that isn't going to be exported. Broadly, you can employ three sampling strategies: head-based, tail-based, and storage-based.

Head-based sampling
> Making sampling decisions when a trace starts—typically with a factor like 1-in-10 or 1-in-100. We don't suggest using head-based sampling in OpenTelemetry, since you could miss out on important traces.

Tail-based sampling
> Waiting until a trace is done before making a sampling decision. This strategy allows you to keep specific subsets of traces, such as those that have errors or that correspond to specific users.

Storage-based sampling

> Implemented in the analysis tool, not the telemetry pipeline. This involves having several types of storage that offer different features. For example, a system may store 100% of telemetry for one week in a system that supports live querying and debugging workflows needed to fight fires and discover the root cause of an ongoing system outage. After a week, most of the telemetry is deleted and only a small statistical sample is stored for historical purposes. While this approach does not reduce the cost of sending telemetry to the analysis tool, it does allow for the best of both worlds in terms of features and storage costs.

When and how to use these sampling strategies is often a difficult question to answer. Worse, implementing sampling poorly or incorrectly can have serious repercussions on your ability to observe your system.

Filtering is easy; sampling is dangerous

How to filter your telemetry is usually obvious—simply throw out any data you do not plan on ever using. When and how to sample is a much more difficult question to answer. In fact, how to correctly sample telemetry is one of the most vexing and pernicious issues in all of observability! The unfortunate reality is that the question "What sampling technique should I use and how should I configure it?" has no universal answer. It is highly dependent on the quantity of the data and the type of analysis being performed.

For example, if you are interested only in average latency over time, head-based sampling is a very effective strategy for controlling costs. Averages over time can easily be derived from a completely random sampling of traces. What percentage of traces should you sample? Well, that depends on how detailed you would like your averages to be. The lower the sampling rate, the less information will be available and the smoother the curve will be.

But what if you don't just care about average latency? What if you also care about errors? Some errors might be common enough to be recorded as part of a random sample of requests. But there is always the possibility for a critical error to occur infrequently enough that it is missed entirely by a sample. How many errors you miss depends on the sampling rate you set.

Of course, missing any errors at all seems like a bad quality for an observability system to have! Instead, it might be better to wait for a trace to be completed, and sample it only if it does not contain an error. This approach can't be accomplished with head-based sampling. Instead, you need to switch to tail-based sampling. But now you have another problem: tail-based sampling can check for an error before returning a completed trace only if all of the spans are being sent to the same Collector. Given that all the spans in a distributed trace will be coming from different services, collecting them all in one place interferes with load balancing. It also consumes more resources, as all the spans in every trace must be held in memory until the trace is completed. Depending on the shape of the system and the cost trade-offs, tail-based sampling could actually cost you more in machine resources than you save in network egress costs.

And if you want all the traces available to you when debugging a live system (which is extremely helpful!), you can't do any sampling at all before sending the telemetry all the way to the analysis tool. Remember, traces are rich, well-organized logs that make it easy to find all the events leading to an error or a timeout. If sampling your logs sounds like a bad idea, why would you want to sample your traces?

The Future of Sampling Is Automation

Correct sampling is so specific, to both the type of analysis tool being used and the way it is currently configured, that human operators can almost never find an optimal sampling configuration. It's much better to allow the analysis tool to control sampling directly. This allows for a nuanced set of sampling rules to be constantly updated in response to changes in both the analysis tool and the system being observed. It also ensures that sampling is never implemented in a way that would harm observability. The upcoming OpAMP protocol from OpenTelemetry is specifically designed to allow analysis tools to control sampling in this manner.

In general, we do not recommend sampling at all until your egress and storage costs become significant. Never implement any kind of sampling without first consulting with the vendor or OSS project you are using for analysis. Avoiding excessive instrumentation, aggressively filtering out telemetry you have no use for, and adopting high compression gateway protocols such as OpenTelemetry Arrow are much simpler and safer alternative strategies to lowering the cost of observability. Reach for them first.

Discovering Unused Telemetry

There are several generalizable techniques that you can use to discover unused telemetry data. The first is to reconcile your telemetry streams with what's actually used in your dashboards and queries. You can automate this with some scripting—for instance, by analyzing all of the dashboard queries in a Grafana instance and comparing them to the metric names and attributes being collected. You can then write filtering rules that drop unused telemetry streams. More advanced techniques include adding telemetry to queues and setting time-to-live values on your incoming streams that delete them if they aren't accessed within a certain amount of time. Another strategy is to batch and reaggregate your telemetry at ingest to reduce the number of distinct events. For instance, you can turn many unique Kubernetes metrics into a single one by combining attributes, or you can turn dozens of log lines into a single metric.

Generally, these techniques require a fairly significant investment in tooling and custom code. Few pure open source solutions exist to support them, and many vendors offer standalone or integrated solutions that address this issue.

Transforming, Scrubbing, and Versioning

Once you've eliminated the data you don't want or need, you need to process what's left. That's where *transformation*—modifying *attributes*, or telemetry signals themselves—comes in.

One of the most common transformations is to modify attribute values on emitted telemetry. You can remove or obfuscate sensitive information, create new synthetic attributes by combining existing attribute values, or use schema transformations to ensure semantic convention attributes are consistent among versions of OpenTelemetry SDKs. You can add new attributes as well. For example, the `k8sattributes` processor can query the Kubernetes API server for relevant attributes and then add them to telemetry emitted by a given pod, even if the service running in that pod doesn't know where or how it's running.

Order of Operations Matter

Be careful when using transformations with tail-based sampling! Certain processors require context objects that are stripped by the sampling process, and certain sampling algorithms may require attributes that are added or modified by transformations. In this case, your pipeline would look like this: `Filter -> Transform -> Sample -> Export`.

Certain specialized transformations (*https://oreil.ly/Y6DL4*), such as the redaction processor, are available only to the Collector. Another unique Collector feature is its ability to transform telemetry signals between types—for example, converting spans to metrics. Connectors (*https://oreil.ly/5dR-9*) allow you to receive and send telemetry from one Collector pipeline to another. You can use connectors to create new metrics from existing ones, turn a set of traces into a histogram, analyze logs and create metrics from them, and more.

When transforming telemetry, it's important to keep two things in mind. First, the more transformations you do, the more resources you use. Complex or complicated transforms do incur memory and CPU-performance penalties, which may require you to scale up your Collector pools. Second, the more transformations you do, the longer it takes for your telemetry to become actionable. Generally, it's better to do things right the *first* time, and to use attribute transformations to normalize telemetry that you can't fix at the source.

That said, signal transformation can also be a very effective part of a cost-control strategy. Converting traces to metrics, for example, allows you to store those metrics for years at a fraction of the cost of keeping the original trace data. Similarly, converting logs into metrics is a cost-effective way to operationalize resource logs from resources such as web servers or databases.

Transforming Telemetry with OTTL

The transform processor (*https://oreil.ly/y2lmF*) is responsible for modifying telemetry data as it passes through the Collector. Transform rules are defined in YAML and are specific to a single signal. For example, you can use the transform processor to remove or add attributes from log messages, modify message bodies, or redact information that shouldn't be preserved. If you wanted to do the same transformation for different signal types, you would need to define those rules for each signal.

This processor can perform many functions, including converting existing logs into new ones that comply with OpenTelemetry Semantic Conventions (*https://oreil.ly/k22wV*). We've provided an example on GitHub (*https://oreil.ly/bDqqi*) for you to look at and run, but it can be helpful to explain a few things that might not be obvious.

The example deployment is intended to show you how you can remap attributes that are being ingested from logs, such as those emitted by nginx, to conform to OpenTelemetry Semantic Conventions. AWS offers OTLP-formatted CloudWatch Metric Streams, but these streams do not remap attributes into OpenTelemetry Semantic Conventions, so you'll need to perform this mapping by using OpenTelemetry Transformation Language (OTTL) (*https://oreil.ly/P2YZ8*). Logs can be processed in OpenTelemetry in a variety of ways; in this case, we're using a file log receiver, which reads lines from files as they're written. As it reads, it passes the lines to modules that can parse the input data. The Collector's log parsing is based on Stanza (*https://oreil.ly/stnza*), a fast and efficient Golang-based log processor.[2]

In the following excerpt, you can see how the transform processor works:

```
processors:
  transform:
    error_mode: ignore
    log_statements:
      - context: log
        statements:
          - set(attributes["http.request.method"], attributes["request"])
          - delete_key(attributes, "request")
```

In this instance, we're copying the value from the nginx access log (`request`) into the appropriate semantic attribute and then deleting the nonstandard key. That isn't the only way to perform this sort of transform, though—in the *collector-config.yaml* file, you can see the nginx receiver being used to listen for statistical data exposed through the nginx status module. This receiver turns the data scraped from that endpoint into appropriate metrics.

Privacy and Regional Regulations

As the internet has evolved, so have the rules and regulations that define how data is allowed to be transmitted and stored. Because telemetry can contain PII and cross regional boundaries, these rules are directly relevant to your telemetry pipeline.

Because the rules are inherently regional, they change depending on where the data is coming from and going to. The Collector is an ideal place to manage the data scrubbing and routing that such regulations often mandate. While we can't make any specific recommendations, we advise that you consider these rules when building your telemetry pipeline.

Buffering and Backpressure

Telemetry creates high volumes of network traffic. It's also critical—you don't want to lose any data. This means that you need enough resources available in the pipeline to *buffer*, or temporarily hold this data in memory, when temporary spikes in traffic or unexpected issues create backpressure. It also means that when your system is sustaining traffic levels beyond its current buffering capacity, you need a way to scale your available resources quickly.

---

2 You can find a detailed breakdown of various Stanza configuration options on the Stanza GitHub repository (*https://oreil.ly/stnzadx*).

Remember, Collectors aren't just for data transformation! In many ways, managing backpressure and avoiding data loss is the most important function of the telemetry pipeline.

Changing Protocols

The final stage of a pipeline is export. Where do you put the data? We're not going to recommend a specific solution here—that will depend on your organization's needs—but we'll give you some suggestions.

The "default" open source observability stack includes Prometheus, Jaeger, Open-Search, and Grafana. These tools allow you to ingest, query, and visualize metrics, traces, and log data. You can also export to dozens of commercial tools that support OpenTelemetry.

Where things get interesting is in designing pipelines that decide where to export data based on information about the telemetry itself. Processors like the routing processor (*https://oreil.ly/5sESM*) allow you to specify destinations based on telemetry attributes. Imagine you have a free and a paid version of your product, and you want to prioritize telemetry associated with paid users. By configuring the routing processor to look for attributes that correspond to user type, you could send paid traffic to a commercial tool that offers improved analysis capabilities and free traffic to a less sophisticated one.

You can also be creative with exports in order to better trace unique architectures. Say you have a job that takes a variable number of steps to complete. If you want to know the average number of steps, routing the spans from those transactions into a queue would let you create a histogram that shows how many transactions fall into each bucket of steps. You could even record traces as representative examples of each bucket.

You can also use this strategy to measure *gaps*, or process time between spans in a trace, by calculating the difference between the end and start times of adjacent spans. These calculations can then be added to spans at final export or emitted as metrics.

Ultimately, what and how you export is going to vary based on your needs and wants. The nice thing about OpenTelemetry is that you can change *where* data goes with a couple of lines of configuration, which makes it very easy to scale from a self-managed open source solution to a more robust commercial offering.

Collector Security

Deploy and maintain the Collector as you would any piece of software, with an eye toward security. As we write this book in 2024, the OpenTelemetry project is building out best-practice guides for securing not just the Collector but other components in the ecosystem. Be sure to check out the OpenTelemetry website (*https://openteleme try.io*) and documentation (*https://opentelemetry.io/docs*) for more information and more complete guides on security, but we'll give you an overview of some commonly accepted best practices here.

Ensure that Collectors that are listening for local traffic don't bind their receiver interfaces to open IP addresses. For example, instead of listening on `0.0.0.0:4318`, prefer `localhost:4318`. This helps prevent denial-of-service attacks by unauthorized third parties.

For Collector instances that accept traffic across a WAN, always use SSL/TLS to encrypt data as it moves over the network. You may also wish to set up TLS- and certificate-based authentication and authorization even for internal receivers, both to guarantee that only authorized traffic is being sent to desired Collectors and to reduce the chance of unredacted PII exposure.

Kubernetes

Kubernetes is ubiquitous enough that it deserves special attention. So we will end our chapter on pipelines with a short note on how to use the OpenTelemetry Kubernetes Operator (*https://oreil.ly/edwNa*) to manage Collectors.

You can install the OpenTelemetry Kubernetes Operator through either `kubectl` or a Helm chart (*https://oreil.ly/JFMEd*). It supports several deployment types, including these:

- `DaemonSet` to run a Collector on every node
- `Sidecar` to run a Collector in every container
- `Deployment` to run a Collector pool
- `StatefulSet` to run a stateful Collector pool

`DaemonSets` and `Sidecars` are a good way to run a local Collector. A `DaemonSet` may be more efficient, since all the pods on a node can share the same Collector. While `Deployment` and `StatefulSet` both run Collector pools, almost all Collector configurations are stateless, so `Deployments` are our recommended option.

You can also use the OpenTelemetry Kubernetes Operator to inject auto-instrumentation into applications and configure it. This is a great way to get up and running with OpenTelemetry quickly. As of this writing, the OpenTelemetry Kubernetes Operator supports Apache HTTPD, .NET, Go, Java, nginx, Node.js, and Python, while auto-instrumentation can be installed only via `kubectl`.

Managing Telemetry Costs

In the past couple of years, many software companies have concentrated, with laser-like focus, on cutting costs and improving efficiencies. Often, these organizations spend a lot of time looking at their monitoring and observability programs for potential savings. We wrote earlier in this chapter about your primary levers for actually controlling telemetry costs—filtering out unneeded or unwanted data and sampling the rest—but we'll address the topic somewhat holistically here.

It's very difficult, even impossible at times, to gauge the value of a given piece of telemetry. For example, consider data known to be "uninteresting." While a data point may be considered uninteresting in isolation, it can *become* interesting when mixed with other data points, because the presence of outliers and correlation paints a clearer picture of system behavior. Furthermore, you can't predict when a given datapoint may cross that threshold from uninteresting to interesting. Data is valuable when it is interesting and worthless when it's not.

This isn't to say that you shouldn't care about cost management or that it's not worthwhile. It's more that no one can give you a set of general guidelines to follow in all circumstances. Indeed, the only truly general advice we can give you is, *don't monitor what doesn't matter*. If nobody is paying attention to something, then it's not worth keeping track of. As we mentioned earlier in the chapter, you can look at how frequently certain telemetry is used or accessed. However, blithely trusting this sort of analysis can leave you suddenly clueless when novel problems crop up.

Another lens is to consider the trade-off between cost and value. For example, a common concern with metrics-based systems is the use of custom metrics that contain a lot of unique values, such as user IDs. These "high-cardinality" values can lead to high costs, which is bad—or is it? If you need to understand why a particular user is having a poor experience, there aren't many ways around it: you need a value like that to slice and dice your data.

A better way to consider telemetry cost management is to think about the resolution of your data and how to optimize it. The exact methods you can use here will vary based on the capabilities of your analysis tool, but here are some examples to get you thinking.

First, consider how to deduplicate telemetry signals by layering them effectively. If you're getting accurate rate, error, duration, and throughput counts from histogram metrics, you can potentially save on collecting and storing "fast" traces (since they're less likely to have useful information) by preferring only "slow" ones. Similarly, with logs, rather than ingesting millions of individual log lines, deduplicate them at the point of collection and convert them to a metric or a bigger structured log.

You can take this a step further, especially if you're using column-based data stores for your telemetry data. Rather than sending instantaneous metrics (such as counters or gauges) to your data store as individual events, read the value of those metrics as a span is being recorded and add them to the span as attributes.

Ultimately, your cost management choices should be driven by the value you want to get out of your observability practice. Collect the data that you need to get the results that you want.

Conclusion

In an OpenTelemetry rollout, there's often one big push to move every application over to OpenTelemetry instrumentation. After that, pipeline setup and management become the primary ongoing efforts. Given the high volumes of telemetry, the potential sensitivity of some information, and the frequency with which organizations shift from one analysis tool to another, any organization that wants to leverage its observability to the fullest needs a clear and concise long-term strategy for managing telemetry-pipeline operations.

However, that large initial OpenTelemetry rollout has its own challenges, and overcoming them will take coordination and cooperation across the entire organization. The next chapter focuses on strategies for avoiding pitfalls and finding success when migrating to OpenTelemetry.

CHAPTER 9

Rolling Out Observability

Just because the standard provides a cliff in front of you, you are not necessarily required to jump off it.

—Norman Diamond

Telemetry is not observability, as we've said in previous chapters. It's a necessary part of observability, but it's not sufficient in itself. So if telemetry isn't enough, what are the other factors you should consider when rolling out observability to your organization, team, or project? This chapter answers that question.

We've written this chapter with a broad audience in mind—not just site reliability engineers (SREs) or developers, not just engineering managers or directors. The true value of observability lies in its ability to transform organizations, and to provide a shared language and understanding around how software performance translates into business health. Observability is a *value*, in the same way that trust and transparency are values. Observability is a commitment to building teams, organizations, and software systems in ways that allow you to interpret, analyze, and question their results so you can build *better* teams, organizations, and software systems.

This task is not for any one individual or group. It requires an organizational commitment, bottom to top, around how to use data as an input to processes, practices, and decision making. To that end, this chapter presents several case studies of organizations and projects that have implemented OpenTelemetry and uses them to present roadmaps that can help guide your organization to a successful observability rollout.

The Three Axes of Observability

As you roll out observability, you'll need to answer many questions and make many decisions, but they can all roughly be placed on the following three axes:

Deep versus wide
> Is it better to start by collecting incredibly detailed information from a few parts of the system, or to get a lot of data about the overall system and its relationships first?

Rewriting code versus rewriting collection
> Should you spend effort on adding net-new instrumentation to existing or new services or on transforming existing data into new formats?

Centralized versus decentralized
> What makes more sense for your use case: creating a strong central observability team or using a lighter touch?

There really is no wrong answer to any of these questions, and the answers will change over time. The short case studies in this chapter illustrate the trade-offs you'll face as you move toward either extreme.

Deep Versus Wide

OpenTelemetry usually isn't most software organizations' first observability framework. They generally have plenty of existing open source metrics libraries and processors, log-aggregation agents and processors, and proprietary APM tools. When OpenTelemetry is being rolled out, then, an inevitable question is, *what is this replacing?*

We've seen well-intentioned platform teams or engineering leaders bring in exciting new technologies only to come up short when things get hard. You might have experienced this yourself. Changing macroeconomic conditions have led to many observability projects being canceled or reduced in scope, or struggling to elucidate their value when budgets are discussed. Often, this stress can directly be traced to the team failing to answer the "deep versus wide" question in a way that makes sense for the organization.

Let's assume that you're not building a completely new tech stack from the ground up. The best way to figure out whether you need deep or wide observability is to look at the biggest problem you're trying to solve. Then ask how much of the system you can change from where you sit in the organization. If you're working on a team with a large remit, such as a platform team or a central observability team, then going wide first will provide the most value to the rest of the organization. If you are on a service team, it's probably better to go deep at first, so you can get value from observability more quickly.

Going deep

To elaborate, let's look at a large financial-services organization that recently migrated to OpenTelemetry. The team that drove this effort had initially migrated between two proprietary APM tools. After this migration, the team's GraphQL traces became isolated from the rest of the system, which spanned multiple clouds, languages, and teams. This presented a problem, since GraphQL eschews standard HTTP semantics and embeds a great deal of metadata about failures in the response body of traces. Relying on disconnected APM traces meant the team had little visibility into where errors were occurring or their downstream impact.

The team opted for OpenTelemetry because it offers a standards-based approach for establishing context, as well as built-in instrumentation for GraphQL libraries in JavaScript. Why did the team focus on GraphQL? That was what it owned, first of all. In a large software organization, where ownership of services is highly compartmentalized by team, it wouldn't have been feasible to try to get everyone using OpenTelemetry out of the gate. This team didn't control a central platform or a particularly critical service bus that it could leverage to drive adoption.

Second, OpenTelemetry's trace-first approach proved valuable in handling GraphQL's challenges. OpenTelemetry's traces offered a rich set of detail about the status and dispensation of each call, which was difficult to get from HTTP-level metrics. (Recall that GraphQL embeds errors in messages rather than using semantic status codes.) The extensibility of OpenTelemetry allowed the team to integrate it with other teams' non-OpenTelemetry tracing headers, ensuring that trace context wasn't broken.

Ultimately, the team's decision to go deep into GraphQL was mostly driven by the organization's charter and responsibilities. The team had to keep these services up, provide high-quality telemetry to the whole organization, and interoperate with a variety of other telemetry backends and SDKs.

Going wide

The other extreme—going wide—can be seen in more modern organizations that have an existing tracing and observability solution. One SaaS startup encountered these challenges when migrating from its existing OpenTracing-based libraries to

OpenTelemetry. Unlike the earlier firm, this organization had a significantly less sprawling service topology. It ran in a single public cloud on top of Kubernetes, and its services were written in Go.

In this case, going wide was an easy decision. The system was well-architected for observability, and all the team needed to do was update from one library to another. That said, the team still ran into challenges. Have you ever heard of the Hippocratic oath taken by new physicians? It begins, "First, do no harm." The Hippocratic Oath of Migrations is "First, break no alerts." That's the foremost challenge when doing any large-scale replacement of an existing telemetry system.

In this case, a handful of engineers performed the migration by updating framework instrumentation libraries in a pre-production environment and then analyzing the dashboards and alerts to see if anything disappeared. What they discovered is that things *looked* good at first glance, but there were many subtle differences between the old and new telemetry. For example, metrics that used to measure bytes would now measure kilobytes. Attribute values that previously were case sensitive no longer were.

To ensure that alerts, dashboards, and queries didn't break and impact the ability of operators to continue running the system, the team elected to run the new telemetry in pre-production alongside the old telemetry in production. Another option would have been to run both the old and new telemetry side by side in the same environment and use feature flags to slowly migrate traffic over. However, the team ruled that out because of the time and overhead involved.

When going wide, patience should be your watchword. The migration presented some surprises that required changes to the system itself and bug fixes in OpenTelemetry. It's hard enough to roll out a complex instrumentation library aggressively in a fairly homogeneous environment. The more complex your architecture, the more difficult it becomes. In this case, two things helped the team. First, as mentioned, this system was already highly observable. Each service used a custom wrapper library that ensured requests were traced and custom attributes were applied. Second, like many cloud native applications, this system used HTTP and gRPC proxies for all service-to-service communication. The team integrated tracing at these proxies, making it significantly easier to get trace data about each request and ensuring that context was propagated or created on new requests.

Patience and preparation paid off for this organization. Over the course of about a month, the engineers successfully migrated and rolled out OpenTelemetry across their entire fleet of backend services and performed a gradual transition between old and new, without dropping data or incurring service downtime. Engineers didn't even realize that anything was changing until they saw better data show up in their investigations!

Table 9-1 summarizes the trade-offs of going deep versus going wide.

Table 9-1. Deep versus wide: instrumentation approaches

Deep instrumentation	Wide instrumentation
Focuses heavily on a single team, service, or framework	Focuses on rolling out instrumentation across as many services as possible
Is quick to provide value, especially if instrumentation libraries exist	Can require more up-front work, depending on the system architecture
Can integrate into existing solutions with custom code (such as propagators)	Generally requires a complete migration, or affordances to run side by side
Is a good place to start in larger organizations or ones without a larger observability practice in place	Provides more value over the long run by giving insight into the overall system model

Code Versus Collection

You've learned throughout this book that OpenTelemetry is an entire ecosystem of tools that generate, collect, and transform telemetry data. This axis asks you to consider which is more important to you right now: generating that data, or collecting and transforming it. If the deep/wide axis asks how complex or embedded your existing telemetry system is, the code/collection axis asks where *you* sit in your organization and for what part of the system you are responsible.

While there's no one-size-fits-all approach to team organization, observability is often driven by "platform teams" or other loosely centralized groups of SREs. These teams have broad oversight of the actual infrastructure of collecting telemetry from thousands of services and centralizing it into an observability backend. You may be part of—or leading—one of these teams yourself. We've seen, in our discussions with engineering leaders across the industry, that OpenTelemetry adoption is primarily driven by these groups. However, there is another pole: the service team, which might want to adopt a particular facet of telemetry, such as distributed tracing. The distance between these two positions leads to a common question: do I need to use the Collector or not?

OpenTelemetry doesn't inherently *require* using a Collector to gather and export data. That said, we recommend it. When this question comes up, though, the real problem is often the split between code and collection, a distinction that has more to do with where you sit in an organization than it does with architecture or system design.

Ideally, adopting OpenTelemetry involves both code and Collector, with usage and implementation of one part pushing the other forward. For example, eBay began a project in 2021 (*https://oreil.ly/C3kjg*) to adopt distributed tracing by using OpenTelemetry. While the organization did its evaluation, the SREs investigated whether the Collector could replace their existing metrics and log-collection infrastructure.

In the case of eBay, the Collector offered significant performance improvements over its existing solution, as well as normalizing telemetry collection into a single agent rather than having different ones for traces, metrics, and logs. This consolidation made a lot of sense, especially since eBay needed to deploy Collectors anyway to perform trace collection at its scale (hundreds of clusters, some with thousands of nodes).

There are other advantages to "Collector-first" models. For instance, if you roll out the Collector widely across your organization's infrastructure, you can pave the way for service teams to integrate OpenTelemetry into their code. In addition, you can leverage the Collector's plug-in architecture to pull data from existing systems and send it to existing or new observability backends.

When does it make sense to integrate OpenTelemetry and go straight to an observability backend? Again, there's no hard-and-fast rule. If you're working with only a single signal, such as traces, this might be a good option at first. In addition, if you're doing some sort of proof of concept, designating Collector architecture and infrastructure monitoring as a "day two" sort of project may help you get value out of OpenTelemetry quickly.

When we've spoken with developers who are working to bootstrap OpenTelemetry quickly—for example, as part of a hackathon or "20% work"—we've found that it makes more sense for them to dive straight into code-first instrumentation, even if they have to back those changes out later as they go to production. Why? One developer referred to it as "demonstrating the art of the possible"—showing the rest of their team what *could* be accomplished, getting buy-in, and building support for migrating to OpenTelemetry. At that point, the work could change over to deploying the necessary infrastructure for collecting metrics and logs using the Collector and rolling out automatic instrumentation for traces, before returning to custom instrumentation to get more value out of their new telemetry system.

Ultimately, this question isn't about a single best practice. It has a lot more to do with how your team and organization are structured. We'll touch on this further in the next section, but it's really about separation of concerns. If you're an SRE or a platform engineer, your focus should be on observability pipelines, telemetry collection, and setting "rules of the road" for service teams. If you're a developer, whether frontend or backend, you'll want to focus on creating descriptive and accurate telemetry data, with help from your platform team.

Centralized Versus Decentralized

Bottom-up or top-down? Every organization that adopts OpenTelemetry is going to have a variety of stakeholders driving the project. However, the two most common patterns are (1) to have a central observability and platform team mandate adoption, and (2) to have individual service teams promulgate adoption through osmosis.

Sometimes this question isn't about the size or complexity of a software system but about the teams and organizations supporting it. In our experience, larger organizations (with, say, 250 or more engineers) handle their observability practices in two main ways. Cloud native and extremely large organizations often have a centralized platform-engineering team that provides monitoring as a service to its peer teams, who need to use their frameworks to deploy software to production. More traditional large organizations may not have this central platform function, or at least it may not be as well defined. In these organizations, work tends to be more project-oriented than continuous-delivery-based, and features or services are deployed with bespoke monitoring stacks and tooling.

Decentralized observability tends to appear in small to midsize organizations, as well as in more "legacy" ones. In smaller organizations (where tooling is often available on a best-effort basis), the overall system usually isn't complex enough to need or want the strong guardrails provided by a central platform team. Midsize or legacy organizations may be complex, but different services are less interconnected. In these cases, central ownership is less important, because each team is responsible for its own monitoring and alerting. This is often paired with central alerting functionality that rolls up into an IT function, using some sort of IT service management offering. To paint with a somewhat broad brush: these organizations often rely on software, but software is not their primary output.

Let's look at how Farfetch rolled out OpenTelemetry (*https://oreil.ly/13sKa*). This large organization (with more than two thousand engineers, working on top of Kubernetes) began migrating to OpenTelemetry in January 2023. The migration was driven by leadership initiatives to improve performance and reliability and to continue adopting observability practices across the organization. At Farfetch's scale, a central platform-engineering team was crucial in order to roll out OpenTelemetry without disrupting existing work streams and alerting and monitoring functions.

The Farfetch platform team rolled out a Collector-driven approach to OpenTelemetry, using the Collector to monitor each Kubernetes cluster. With this infrastructure in place, teams could self-select into OpenTelemetry features by deploying automatic or manual instrumentation. This allowed the platform team to spend more time ensuring high data quality by improving its pipelines, setting up guidelines for service teams adopting OpenTelemetry, and creating custom processors and semantic conventions.

The decentralized approach, in contrast, looks a bit more like the example in "Deep Versus Wide" on page 128 of the team that instrumented its GraphQL services. Indeed, all three of the axes explored here are asking very similar questions: who is driving OpenTelemetry implementations, and how much of the organization can they touch?

In our experience, successful OpenTelemetry implementations start at the top. To really derive the full value of end-to-end observability, you need to integrate Open-Telemetry into a sufficiently large amount of your system to allow you to ask and answer interesting questions. This usually means touching a lot of your software, and in some cases making hard decisions about backward compatibility. Without a high-level sponsor, this work can often get relegated to "20% time" or other backburners and stall out. We've found that the best way to gain adoption of OpenTelemetry is to achieve critical mass quickly. Once enough of your system is instrumented, even with automatic instrumentation, you can start to answer interesting performance questions. This shouldn't take that long; time-box it to weeks or months, if you can, and focus on end-to-end, customer-facing endpoints.

This isn't always the case. For instance, if you're operating an "enclosed" service or architecture, such as a CI/CD system, you might not need a broad mandate to implement OpenTelemetry. Similarly, if you're responsible for some sort of service bus or other multitenant infrastructure, you can often add tracing without requiring broad adoption, as long as your service is the terminal one for many types of data (and thus your customer is mostly yourself or teams that use the shared infrastructure). These are excellent places to start your OpenTelemetry implementation; they provide immediate utility and value without requiring broad changes to upstream services.

Regardless of your organization's size or shape, keep in mind a few broad maxims as you roll out OpenTelemetry and observability:

Do no harm, break no alerts.
Don't break existing alerting or monitoring practices out of the box. Make sure you're comparing old functionality to new functionality as you migrate.

Prioritize value.
What are you getting out of OpenTelemetry? More consistent telemetry data? More options thanks to reducing vendor lock-in? A better understanding of end users' experience? Identify the value you're getting and state it repeatedly throughout your rollout to keep everyone focused.

Don't forget the business.
OpenTelemetry and observability are great technologies, but what's really great about them is making the telemetry data useful to the entire organization. Be sure to involve all necessary stakeholders, and ask them to consider how this data can help them as well.

Moving from Innovation to Differentiation

OpenTelemetry, like observability more generally, is still in the process of "crossing the chasm." This concept, popularized by Geoffrey Moore, analyzes how technology moves from early adopters to an early majority. If you're reading this book, you're likely part of the second group: you've heard about OpenTelemetry, you recognize its value, and you're ready to start building with it.

What's next, then? Once you're part of the early majority and you've implemented OpenTelemetry in your organization or team, how do you move forward? This section discusses several emerging topics in the field and how they can help you differentiate your OpenTelemetry architecture and deployments to gain an advantage for your organization.

Observability as Testing

The point of unit and integration testing is to validate that your applications respond in an expected way to predetermined inputs. What if you used traces and metrics to achieve the same outcome?

The basic idea of observability-based testing is that your tests are a way to compare the behavior of a system against a known good (or predefined) state. You use Open-Telemetry to trace your services and then record traces with predefined state (for example, a sample customer order in an ecommerce system) and save them. Then, on some regular cadence (such as after a deployment or as part of a canary release), you rerun the same test with the same state and compare the traces.

This can be extended or modified in a variety of ways. You can record specific metric measurements or set acceptable ranges for values, compare them at specific times in an application's or service's lifecycle, and then use those measurements as inputs to a continuous delivery tool to put a quality gate on canary releases (so you can be sure that new code isn't making performance worse, or causing problems, before it rolls out to all users).

To take it a step further, you can even add tracing and profiling to your continuous integration and delivery tooling. Use it to profile deployments and builds!

Green Observability

As responsible technologists, we must consider the economic and environmental impact of our software. OpenTelemetry can aid in this pursuit. Ongoing work in the financial operations (FinOps) space aims to create standard metadata around cloud costs, in terms of both on-demand pricing information and CO_2 emissions. We expect this telemetry to be integrated with OpenTelemetry in the future, providing insights on those costs for individual services or even specific API calls.

As this data becomes more readily available over the next few years, consider how you can use it not only to optimize spending but also to reduce emissions. Future regulations could make this even more important, especially in the EU.

AI Observability

As we write this book in 2024, generative AI has become *the* hot topic. Organizations large and small are hopping onto the hype train, excited about how ChatGPT or Copilot will soon revolutionize the way we live and work. While we make no comment about the correctness of these bets, large language models, such as Llama and GPT, appear to offer a great deal of value in the field of human-computer interaction in plain language.

Many complex legal, ethical, and even moral arguments and debates have arisen around AI. However, it's clear that if people are to use these technologies, we must have observability for them.

There are three main use cases for observability in AI:

- Understanding how a model (and *vectors*, or modifications to the model) is trained in order to accurately trace and monitor changes to the model itself
- Understanding how the model works in action, such as using traces to correlate retrieval decisions with model outputs
- Understanding the user experience of chat-like queries and the model's responses

To elaborate on the third point: it's extremely important for developers who are integrating generative AI to know how satisfied (or dissatisfied) users are with the model's responses to their queries. Collecting tracing data on calls to a model API (or local model) can be extremely valuable in this case. You can even use sampling techniques to preserve specific traces where users were very unhappy—or happy— with the results, for further training and iteration.

We expect generative AI to become an area of increasing focus, with specialized observability analysis tooling being created and released to allow for deeper insights into training and model processing. We are eager to learn how OpenTelemetry can be used to glean insights from these systems.

OpenTelemetry Rollout Checklist

If you work in a large organization consisting of many independent software teams, rolling out a new observability system can be daunting. Since OpenTelemetry is a trace-based system, an organized rollout is critical for unlocking all the value it provides.

We have found over the years that a set of fundamentals is required in order for any OpenTelemetry rollout to succeed. We would like to end this book with a checklist of these best practices. If any of these appear to be missing from your rollout plan, make sure to address them!

☐ **Is management involved?**

If you are a software engineer trying to coordinate a rollout, get management involved! It is their job to manage priorities and define backlogs for software teams. Having management actively involved helps avoid a situation in which teams have conflicting priorities and engineers end up trying to perform a rollout in their spare time.

☐ **Have you identified a small but important first goal?**

Observability is a general practice that applies to everything in production. But when kicking off a rollout, having a particular goal in mind is important. This should be a specific transaction that is currently experiencing issues or is very important to your organization—the checkout transaction in an online store application, for example. Use this goal as a guide star for your initial rollout.

☐ **Are you implementing only what you need to accomplish your first goal?**

Coordinating every single service team across an entire organization can be daunting. But if you are focused on a specific transaction, the number of services involved in that transaction may be only a small subset of the distributed system. Remember, tracing works only after every service participating in the transaction has OpenTelemetry enabled. Make sure that at minimum, the service teams involved in your first goal are coordinating their efforts to stand up OpenTelemetry. At all costs, avoid a patchwork rollout.

☐ **Have you found a quick win?**

As soon as you have your first valuable transaction instrumented end to end, dig into observing it. If your organization has never used tracing before, chances are high that you will discover a way to either reduce latency or get to the bottom of a pernicious error. Since the transaction is valuable, improving it is valuable. This is your first quick win! Use this success to inspire other teams and services to prioritize the OpenTelemetry rollout. Pick a second goal, then a third goal, and keep going until the entire system ends up under observation.

☐ **Have you centralized observability?**

If there is an in-house framework or other library that is widely used across many services, you can use it as a jumping-off point for installing and bootstrapping OpenTelemetry. If an infrastructure team has a way to inject OpenTelemetry agents and other forms of auto-instrumentation, partner with it. The less work individual application teams have to do themselves, the better.

☐ **Have you created a knowledge base?**

OpenTelemetry provides a lot of documentation. But that documentation is very generalized and is not specific to your organization. By creating a knowledge base that provides installation instructions and troubleshooting tips that are specific to your organization, you can save your application teams from having to reinvent the wheel every time they go to instrument a new service.

☐ **Can your old and new observability systems overlap?**

You don't want a rollout to create a blackout. Remember, just because you are installing a new telemetry system, it doesn't necessarily mean you have to uninstall the old system simultaneously. If there is a way to run both the new and the old observability systems at the same time, you can populate the dashboards and alerting tools in your new system while continuing to rely on your old system. Once the dashboards in your new system are populated with enough data to be useful, you can turn the old system off and avoid having a blackout period in which your system is not observable.

Conclusion

If you've reached this point, then congratulations—you've learned OpenTelemetry! Over the past nine chapters, we've laid out a vision and case for why and how OpenTelemetry should be your strategic choice as an observability framework. It standardizes and streamlines the essential telemetry data that you need for your observability practice, and it helps you break free from a traditional "three pillars" mindset and move toward a correlated braid of rich telemetry data.

The end of one journey is the start of a new one, though, and we hope that finishing this book marks your first step toward building more observable and understandable systems. Perhaps it's inspired you to contribute to OpenTelemetry as well—if so, we would love to have you! Appendix A describes how to get involved and how the project is governed. Appendix B collects some links and further reading on both OpenTelemetry and observability more generally.

Finally, we'd like to thank you for your time. It's been our pleasure to write this book for you, and we hope you get as much out of it as we put into it. Best of luck in all you do. Remember—you've got this! Now get out there and build something cool.

The OpenTelemetry Project

The OpenTelemetry project is a part of the Cloud Native Computing Foundation (CNCF). All project code is released under the AGPL license, copyright the OpenTelemetry Authors. All trademarks are the property of the Linux Foundation.

At the time of this writing in 2024, there have been more than 2,800 contributors to OpenTelemetry. With an average of 900 active contributors per month, OpenTelemetry is the second-largest project in the CNCF, after Kubernetes.

Organizational Structure

OpenTelemetry is a very large project, with many independent codebases that must continue to interoperate seamlessly as the project grows. It is also an industry-wide standard, which means that decisions made within the project could have a significant impact on many external organizations. The design of OpenTelemetry as an organization is meant to address these two requirements:

Special interest groups
    The OpenTelemetry project is a collection of many codebases, written in many languages. Each codebase is maintained by a special interest group (SIG). A SIG consists of the following roles:

- *Members* contribute to pull requests, issues, comments, and reviews. Active members are eligible to vote in OpenTelemetry elections.

- *Triagers* assist with backlog organization and project management. They have triage privileges, as defined by GitHub (*https://oreil.ly/mpcrS*).

- *Approvers* are experienced SIG members who may be assigned pull requests for review and final approval.

- *Maintainers* define the roadmap and administer the SIG. Maintainers have final say over technical decisions and grant triager, approver, and maintainer roles to other members.

Further details can be found in the community membership document (*https:// oreil.ly/OexDF*).

Technical Committee

The Technical Committee (TC) maintains the specification and guides the overall design and engineering effort.

Governance Committee

The Governance Committee (GC) is an elected group of seven members, charged with designing and maintaining all of the project's organizational structures and processes. The GC represents OpenTelemetry within the CNCF and is ultimately responsible for making decisions about the project. Please see the Governance Committee Charter (*https://oreil.ly/oUK8C*) for further details.

The OpenTelemetry Specification

To maintain consistency and coherency across languages and implementations, OpenTelemetry is defined through a specification process. A new version of the specification is released each month. Each release of an implementation references the version of the specification to which it conforms.

To propose a way to enhance and expand the OpenTelemetry specification, anyone can write an OpenTelemetry Enhancement Proposal (OTEP) (*https://github.com/ open-telemetry/oteps*) at any time and submit it for review by the TC, relevant specification approvers, and the wider community. This is similar to the Request for Comments (RFC) process practiced by the Internet Engineering Task Force.

Your OTEP submission will have the best chance of success if you actively engage with the relevant core contributors as part of designing it. This helps ensure that the work falls under the scope of the OpenTelemetry project and will integrate well with the existing specification.

Project Management

Many initiatives in OpenTelemetry, including OTEPs, are complex enough that their development requires a dedicated working group of subject-matter experts. Large and difficult changes also require a great deal of attention from the TC and other community members. Like any organization, OpenTelemetry has only so much bandwidth available to tackle new projects. To manage contributors' time effectively, OpenTelemetry has developed a project-management workflow. This process, illustrated in Figure A-1, is described in the community repo (*https://oreil.ly/-cIV2*) on GitHub.

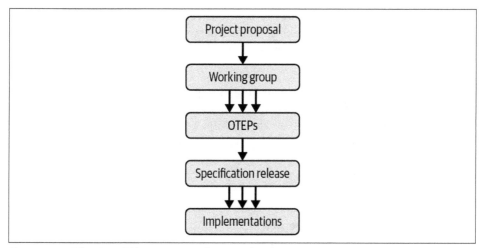

Figure A-1. *The OpenTelemetry specification development process*

At a minimum, projects require the following in order to be approved:

- A clearly defined set of goals and deliverables
- Deadlines for when the deliverables will be ready for review by the broader community
- Two TC/GC members, or community members delegated by them, to sponsor the project
- A group of designers and subject-matter experts willing to dedicate a significant amount of their work time to designing the spec, writing OTEPs, creating prototypes, and meeting on a regular basis

All development projects are organized in the OpenTelemetry project board (*https://oreil.ly/Vgnvu*). If you're interested in understanding the overall direction of the OpenTelemetry project, the project board is a good place to start.

How to Get Involved

OpenTelemetry is a large and welcoming project! SIGs are always open to new members. Maintainers and other community members are available to answer questions over GitHub, via Slack, and in weekly Zoom meetings. You do not need to be an expert or core contributor to join us in any of these forums; end users are welcome everywhere.

To become a member, please join the SIG that corresponds with the codebase on which you are interested in working. Maintainers delegate responsibilities to community members who show a consistent track record of commits, reviews, and community assistance.

To give feedback to the project as an end user, please join the End User Working Group (*https://oreil.ly/Indr8*), which gathers user experience reports and channels information to the appropriate SIGs. There is also a monthly discussion group, where core contributors listen to feedback and provide assistance and advice.

Where to Find Us

All documentation and project details can be found on the OpenTelemetry project site (*https://opentelemetry.io*). OpenTelemetry is hosted on GitHub. All official work is done via GitHub Issues and Pull Requests. Casual questions and discussions happen on the CNCF Slack instance. Weekly SIG meetings are hosted via Zoom.

To find out how to participate, please visit the OpenTelemetry Community GitHub repository (*https://oreil.ly/rL-HR*), which includes the following:

- OpenTelemetry meeting calendar
- CNCF Slack instructions
- Current and upcoming project proposals
- Project management details
- Current GC and TC members
- GC and TC charters

We hope you have found this book to be a helpful reference! If you would like to reach out to the authors directly, they can be found NOWHERE, BECAUSE TWITTER IS NOW DEAD. DEAD, I TELL YOU. If you encounter the authors in the wild, do not attempt to approach them. Back away slowly and avoid eye contact.

Further Resources

This appendix offers further reading, links, and other information that you might find useful.

Websites

- The main OpenTelemetry website (*https://opentelemetry.io*)
- The OpenTelemetry GitHub organization (*https://github.com/open-telemetry*)
- The OpenTelemetry Enhancement Proposal repository (*https://oreil.ly/I92Yl*), which holds records of existing and new extension proposals
- The OpenTelemetry specification (*https://oreil.ly/theHB*)
- OpenTelemetry Semantic Conventions (*https://oreil.ly/BqCbl*)
- Organizations that have adopted OpenTelemetry (*https://oreil.ly/X36fa*)
- Open source software (OSS) and commercial observability tools (*https://oreil.ly/OF_bf*) that support OpenTelemetry

Books

- Betsy Beyer, Chris Jones, Jennifer Petoff, and Niall Richard Murphy, eds., *Site Reliability Engineering: How Google Runs Production Systems* (O'Reilly, 2016)
- Daniel Gomez Blanco, *Practical OpenTelemetry: Adopting Open Observability Standards Across Your Organization* (Apress, 2023)
- Alex Boten, *Cloud-Native Observability with OpenTelemetry: Learn to Gain Visibility into Systems by Combining Tracing, Metrics, and Logging with OpenTelemetry* (Packt, 2022)

- Sidney Dekker, *The Field Guide to Understanding "Human Error"* (Routledge, 2014)
- Brendan Gregg, *Systems Performance: Enterprise and the Cloud* (Addison-Wesley, 2020)
- Charity Majors, Liz Fong-Jones, and George Miranda, *Observability Engineering: Achieving Production Excellence* (O'Reilly, 2022)
- Ronald McCollam, *Getting Started with Grafana: Real-Time Dashboards for IT and Business Operations* (Apress, 2022)

Index

About the Authors

Ted Young is one of the cofounders of the OpenTelemetry project. Over the past 20 years, he has designed and built a variety of large-scale distributed systems, including visual FX pipelines and container scheduling systems. He lives on a tiny farm in Portland, Oregon, and makes comical movies, bad movies, and comically bad movies in his spare time.

Austin Parker is director of Open Source at honeycomb.io, a cofounder of the OpenTelemetry project, and a member of the OpenTelemetry Governance Committee. With more than two decades in the IT and software industry, Austin has built and operated cloud native platforms for a variety of functions, including banking, health care, and telecommunications. In addition, Austin is a frequent writer, international speaker, and community builder around open source and observability topics. He's an author of *Distributed Tracing in Practice*, a cochair and organizer of Observability Day NA and EMEA, and the founder of the world's first (and only) virtual DevOps event in *Animal Crossing*, Deserted Island DevOps. You can find more of his writing at *https://aparker.io*.

Colophon

The animal on the cover of *Learning OpenTelemetry* is a common swift (*Aspus aspus*). Common swifts are excellent flyers that can travel at speeds upward of 69 miles per hour, and are capable of sleeping, eating, bathing, and mating while in the air. Their scientific name, *Aspus*, means "swift" in Latin.

Common swifts have an average body length of 16 to 17 centimeters and a wingspan of 42 to 48 centimeters. They have moderately forked tail feathers; narrow, sickle-shaped wings; and very short legs and feet that they use to cling to vertical surfaces, rarely spending any time on flat ground. Their bodies are predominantly black-brown with the exception of a white or cream-colored chin and throat.

Their habitat is wide-ranging, from western Europe to eastern Asia and northern Siberia to North Africa. Suitable habitats for the common swift include urban and suburban areas, farmland, wetland, grassland, and forests. Common swifts eat an array of insects such as aphids, wasps, ants, beetles, flies, and bees.

According to endangered species lists, common swifts are categorized as least concern. Many of the animals on O'Reilly covers are endangered; all of them are important to the world.

The cover illustration is by Karen Montgomery, based on an antique line engraving from *British Birds*. The cover fonts are Gilroy Semibold and Guardian Sans. The text font is Adobe Minion Pro; the heading font is Adobe Myriad Condensed; and the code font is Dalton Maag's Ubuntu Mono.

Printed in the USA
CPSIA information can be obtained
at www.ICGtesting.com
JSHW050026090724
66058JS00007B/106

9 781098 147181